and then there was *me*

SLOAN ROGERS

living with

a dying

loved one

and then there was *me*

a memoir

TATE PUBLISHING & *Enterprises*

Published by Tate Publishing & Enterprises, LLC
127 E. Trade Center Terrace | Mustang, Oklahoma 73064 USA
1.888.361.9473 | www.tatepublishing.com

Tate Publishing is committed to excellence in the publishing industry. The company reflects the philosophy established by the founders, based on Psalm 68:11,
"The Lord gave the word and great was the company of those who published it."

Book design copyright © 2011 by Tate Publishing, LLC. All rights reserved.
Cover design by Kellie Southerland
Interior design by Nathan Harmony
Author Photo by James Michael Photography

Published in the United States of America

ISBN: 978-1-61739-852-0
1. Biography & Autobiography: Personal Memoirs
2. Family & Relationships: Eldercare
11.01.25

Dedication

In dedication to the *spirit* of *Richard*
Richard W. Rogers
August 2, 1935 to January 16, 2007

My dear Richard, had it not been for our journey, as painful as it was, I would not have been left with a happening to share that will hopefully shed light unto others.

Your departure from this life left me in a state of great numbness but also with the tenacity, with the perseverance, and with the faith that supported our beings.

I was gifted, through a very special life, the opportunity to move forward and truly discover what being alive is all about with a level of passion I would have never thought possible.

My heart is so grateful!

From this point forward, I will be referring to Richard as *Dick* or *D* as I affectionately called him.

Acknowledgments

I know clearly where to start my list, but where to end it is a different matter.

The Lord is my Light, the Lord is my Strength; my Lord dwells within and gives me peace.

Heartfelt thanks and love to my parents, Stephen and Frances Sloan for bringing me into this life and imparting the belief that I should have courage of my convictions. Mom, you are a survivor too. I guess I got it from you, as you will be ninety-eight years young when this story is published. And Dad, despite your early demise, you survived a great deal, with never a complaint, before leaving us. Perseverance prevailed.

To my engaging and loved sisters, twin Raina and sister Dawn, you are there for me, morning, noon, and night time too, with support, with counter thoughts, with honest exchange clearly portraying whose best interest you have at heart. This makes me grateful, blessed, and delighted to say you are *my* sisters. I treasure our mutual love.

Raina, a special thanks for your actual presence when there were many nights I didn't know how I would make it home from different health establishments, but I would blink and there you were. This was certainly a testament to actions speaking louder than words. You did it in a way of not allowing me to say I didn't need help, because you knew I did. How special is that! How wonderfully special you are! Rick, my heartfelt thanks to you for your ever presence with Raina and the comfort I derived in knowing I could count on you as various needs arose—and they did. You lightened my burden.

My wonderfully dynamic and loved children, Stephen and Richard, you have been the light of my life. There is no greater gift. While clearly we need to be there for our children, in the later years when the going got rough, you both were there for me and for Dick of your own volition. Your support, your prayers, your ever presence reaching out in countless ways I couldn't even have fathomed, throughout a long journey, just tells me how very exceptional you each are. I already knew that and further recognize how very blessed I am to have the gift of your lives in mine. God is so good.

My lovely and loved daughters-in-law, Kim (Stephen) and Joan (Richard), I really would like to drop the "in-law."

My life is so much richer for your presence. You both have been more than wonderful to me and supportive to your husbands when the need arose. In some cases, you perceived a need I didn't even know I had until I received your help. Do you know how huge that is? I do, and I will be forever grateful and feel blessed that you are a part of our family.

My delightful and loved grandchildren, Derek and Brandon, you have been star lights in my life. There is something about each of you that brightens my world in a most incredible way. Regardless of the dynamics of a situation, your presence spells hope for the future. Derek and Brandon, you mean the world to me and have brought me great joy and love over the years. Derek, your caring, quiet presence at Pop's funeral had a way of embracing me wonderfully and will never be forgotten. That was your expressed desire, and I want you to know I felt you reaching out to give me extra support—and you did.

My caring and loved stepchildren: I've never liked the word "step"; certainly our language should have an alternative that sounds more loving, as you truly are. In order of age: Bruce, Tracey (and Trey), and Richard, *and* two delightful and loved grandchildren, Jordan and Bryant (the IV), known to Pop Pop as *J-Girl* and *Quarter*, you have brought me such pleasure. This journey was especially significant to you, Bruce, Tracey, and Richard, being Dick's children who he lovingly referred to as, "my guys" (*B.A.R.*, *Girlfriend*, and *Poco*). I can truly say we made the journey together, for all major and often not-so-major decisions were shared. Your welcoming hearts made the process much easier for me as we deliberated, reminisced, and cried together. You were there for me each step of the way. I was touched, and I will always hold you close in my heart. I hope each of you will always know how much I honored your relationship with the man I married, your dad, your Pop Pop.

To Dick's siblings whom I have not stopped thinking of as my brothers and sisters, Lemuel (Gloria), Tom, Bob (Maureen), Diane, Bill (Fern), Peter (Anita), thank you for each caring thought and action.

Diane, it would be remiss of me not to mention how you strengthened my spirit with your love and tremendous faith. How you shared hours with me, watching Dick wrestling to survive major surgery, and I will never forget your driving a total of eleven hours to find yourself coming back to spend another week. Words will never express the gratefulness I felt in my heart when I saw you at my door, saying, "I just couldn't leave you now." I know that you and I both knew that God was at work.

To Dick's brothers, you are each remembered caringly for the kind and wonderful acts you contributed in helping me move through this experience. Lem, for sharing your medical expertise, your many calls, your visits, and particularly your dedication to seeing us through our Bridgeport, Connecticut, experience; Tom, for your presence, support, and for only being a phone call away during our journey; Bob for your presence and offering to help Dick at his office; Bill for your calls and visits; Pete, for your presence and extra support when the end was approaching.

To all the above, I love each and every one of you in a very special way.

To Dick's and my church family, Siloam Baptist Church, pastored by Rev. John H. West III, your constant prayers, outreach of ministries, countless visits, phone calls, and cards … oh, my heart will be forever grateful. I must mention the Male Chorus that ministered to Dick in such a special way, his having been one of the group. What a blessing it was for me to watch the response when you visited, and I do believe that Dick's last spoken phrase was in song: such music to my ears. Siloam, you certainly gave me a testimony.

Valley View Community Church family, pastored by Bruce Carter, my other church home when I needed to be spending more time with my husband, as you had a 9:00 a.m. service, offered me much support and countless prayers as well as a church home away from my church home, where I was embraced by many caring hearts. How blessed I was.

I would be negligent not to mention the Gwynedd Square Nursing Home that was Dick's last home, where he was treated with the utmost dignity and care as he lived out his final days, along with the caring and dedicated support of North Penn Hospice. Between work and home to sleep, I felt like I lived at Gwynedd and got to experience the enrichment they added to a patient's life. That gave me the peace I needed to be able to put my head on my pillow each evening and sleep.

ACTS Retirement-Life Communities, where I am employed and spend many hours a week, your employees exude the most caring hearts I have ever witnessed in a work environment. What rays of sunshine have been shed on my life by a far-reaching staff. Again, I am blessed and grateful.

Elisa, your counseling skills are the best; your observations, your ability to bring focus where needed, your attentive spirit, and your compassion have brought immeasurable value to this period of my life.

Dick had many exceptional doctors and nurses along this journey, too many to name. However, Dr. William Rodgers, since deceased, caringly called me most evenings as I was driving home from Thomas Jefferson Hospital to check on Dick's status and answer any questions I might have. How grateful I was for the comfort this brought me.

Additionally, there are countless, literally countless, individuals that were there for me. I am reluctant to print names in fear of overlooking a special soul. So I extend my heartfelt thanks and wish for endless blessings to each and everyone who in any way walked with Dick and me on our journey. There are some who are in this category that will specifically see themselves depicted in "our" story.

I am further blessed to be working with an exceptional publishing company, Tate Publishing. Their style gives you such assurance that what they say will happen does happen. The process is so well planned. It provides you a true sense of confidence and peace. My editor, Kalyn, is a delight to work with; so dependable. I feel she has a real command of editing, makes such sense, and provides me with references to support her recommendations. She cares and it shows. I know with her efforts my book will be the very best that it can be. All my contacts at Tate have been exceptional.

In final acknowledgment, I want to express my gratitude to you my family and special friends who have encouraged me to write this book. You have listened endlessly, made helpful suggestions, and/or read and re-read my manuscript. To my loving sister Dawn for your tireless efforts, and my special friend Colleen, you both have so caringly shared your unique talents and precious time in giving much added support and suggestions throughout the formative stages of my book. You have all rendered me forever thankful.

Table of Contents

Introduction

Care giving is a journey most of us will face if we live long enough and, for some of us, regardless of how long we don't live. My purpose is to depict how one can rise to meet what life brings his or her way with strength, confidence, grace, and hope.

A statement read at Dick's remembrance service sums it up. A message to "Brother-In-Law" from "Shelbs" (known by most as "Raina"):

> To those of you who mourn Dick
> Rogers, my brother-in-law,
> affectionately called that by me
> since he came into our family,

I simply would like to share
my heart's message with you.
When you want a dose of courage—
think of brother-in-law,
When you want a dose of tenacity—
think of brother-in-law,
When you want a dose of strength—
think of brother-in-law,
When you want a dose of faith—
think of brother-in-law.
He truly embodied these characteristics
of God and many more.
And when you want a dose of love—
think of Sloan.
She was truly his earth angel,
and when he carefully and caringly
looked at Sloan in his final minutes,
you knew he knew this; it
was written in his eyes.
Why, even a nurse at the center said,
"I thought there was someone
very special in that room as I watched
his wife day in and day out
devotedly caring for her husband,
this man called Dick Rogers."

The last six years of his life, Dick's health suffered due to different illnesses and health complications. The individual symptoms of these health problems overlapped and often caused other health issues to recur, creating entirely new problems. Because of the overlapping health complications, our story has been set up according to the most remarkable events that occurred, not according to chronological order. These events were remarkable not only because of the nature of the incidents, but because of the questions that ensued, determinations that were made, and associated wisdom that surfaced. Each chapter focuses on a specific topic with related events described, regardless of when those individual events occurred during the six years preceding D's death. Every chapter contains challenging questions, expressions of faith, and suggestions to ponder. My prayer is that our journey will add something meaningful to your life.

As you read this account of a very determined and courageous man, it might help to have a picture of the progression of that which depleted his life.

In 1969 Dick was in a car accident, hit from behind, that weakened the condition of his cervical spine. By 1978 he was diagnosed with severe spinal stenosis of the cervical cord with myelopathy and spinal arthritis. In part due to the accident and in part due to his natural physical makeup. Spinal stenosis is a narrowing of the spaces in the spine resulting in compression of the nerve roots or spinal cord. So the effects are wide spread depending on the exact area of impingement. The cervical area usually affects the arms and legs.

That same year, Dick underwent a serious laminectomy at Thomas Jefferson. A laminectomy, in simple terms, is a procedure to remove the lamina and spinous process to give the spinal cord more room. After some time of recuperation and being on a five-point walker, he graduated to his normal life style except for an unsteady gait at times.

In 1980 Dick had another car accident, again hit from behind, that caused a marked decline in his condition. By 1988 he had severe stenosis of the cervical canal from C1 to C6. His cord was severely compressed. C1 to C6 is the entire cervical area of the spine.

By 1990 Dick's unsteadiness in balance was causing him to fall. Months turned into weeks and weeks into days in between falls. Unless you happened to be present, you would never know he fell. It was not information he would share after the fact. You simply would not be privy to such a happening, except by a possible observer's comment. The doctor's impression of Dick was that of a quadraparetic, one with very compromised mobility. However, he was still moving through life tirelessly with major determination without anyone being aware of the extent of his mental and physical pain.

This leads up to the first happening of the book, which signaled the beginning of the end. The following is the chronological time line for those occurrences mentioned in subsequent chapters.

June 2000, due to a fall, Dick was in Bridgeport Hospital, Connecticut, suffering seizures that would plague him for the next six years until his death.

August 2000, Dick exhibited memory difficulties.

In 2001, Dick started taking Aricept and a little later Namenda, medications significant for treating Alzheimer's, though also used to treat general memory loss, which I discovered long after the fact.

March 29, 2001, Dick had a corpectomy at Johns Hopkins to remove three vertebra from his cervical spine and fusion with instrumentation. He was in a structured collar, which provided cervical spine immobilization, for three months then to a soft sponge one for an additional three months. He was so relieved not to have a halo brace, which is secured to the skull with pins.

In April 2001, it was apparent that Dick's memory was still declining slightly, and we felt in part it may have been due to the ten-hour surgery.

By May 2001, we were seeing a little progress; however, when we went back to Hopkins for continued review, Dick's gait had worsened. It was thought to have been aggravated by a couple previous seizures.

In November of 2003, Dick went to a driving program at a local rehab center to determine his driving abilities due to his slowing reflexes. It was felt not only due to the seizures but his worsening physical condition that driving needed to be curtailed.

In March of 2004, Dick underwent another ten-hour surgery at Thomas Jefferson Hospital to in effect redo what had been done at Johns Hopkins, only this time using bone graft in place of the instrumentation. This surgery resulted in three months of confinement; a month each in the hospital, rehabilitation at Brywn Mawr Rehab, and at Saunders nursing home.

By May 2006, after many months of anguish, Dick was back and forth between Temple Hospital and Gwynedd Square Nursing Home. What he experienced were infections, falls, hematomas, seizures, more surgery, more memory loss, not to mention the pain of indignities and the loss of self.

Prologue

*And so it was a long
eight months …*

We were a couple that shared many things by default, but when it came to personal feelings, that was rare in any regard. Standing out in my mind, never to be forgotten because it was one of those rare times, was a day in mid-May 2006, just eight months before my husband departed from this world. The moment was profound, the words deep-felt, it chilled my soul.

I had a very determined husband who suffered enormously over the six-year period leading up to May of 2006. Dick's awareness that he was slowly, maybe not so slowly, losing grip of his abilities and faculties was not easy to assimilate, especially for one who always appeared to be in total control of his life. Life became an enormous challenge topped with an unbelievable level of determination for him and a totally revealing test of faith and strength for me.

Dick was a skillful African-American trial attorney who had successfully served his community and fellow man during his career. Why do I mention African-American? It was stated in a very profound *Franklin & Marshall College* magazine cover story that Dick had been raised to believe that whatever he did, he had to do it twice as good to reap the advantages. Perhaps that gives you some idea of the energy and perseverance that was a part of his being, the very fiber that made him tick.

The following will give you some idea of his achievements.

- In junior high, he was the first black president of the student council.

- As a high school junior, he won a national oratorical contest sponsored by the Elks, returning home with a trophy and scholarship.

- When he graduated high school in 1953, he was senior class treasurer and a member of the student council as well as a class officer all three years.

- He enrolled in Franklin & Marshall College as one of fewer than ten students of color in 1953, and in the autumn of 2003, F&M recognized

Dick as a pioneer on campus during the '50s and '60s.

- In 1957, he was admitted to the "Black Pyramid" Senior Honor Society

- After college, Dick served his country by enlisting in the navy.

- In 1960, after an honorable discharge from naval services, Dick entered Dickinson School of Law and earned his Juris Doctor in 1962.

- In 1963, he was admitted to practice law in the Commonwealth of Pennsylvania and did so for more than forty-five years, recognizing his passion.

- He was admitted to the United States Supreme Court, US Court of Appeals for the third circuit, US District Court for the Eastern District of Pennsylvania, US Tax Court, Supreme Court of Pennsylvania, and the Court of Common Pleas and Orphan's Court of Montgomery County, Pennsylvania.

- From 1970 to 1979, Dick was regional counsel for the Pennsylvania State Education Association (PSEA) and successfully argued one of the landmark Pennsylvania cases establishing the rights of women to return to the workplace following a pregnancy.

- He was a longtime board member of the two-hundred-year-old Pennsylvania Prison Society, the oldest reform group in the United States.

- In 1974, Dick was appointed by Governor Milton Shapp and confirmed by legislature for a full six-year term on the Pennsylvania Board of Pardons.

- Every year Dick sponsored a table of ten at the Martin Luther King Jr. Luncheon in Philadelphia. He was such an advocate for justice. Dick passed away early in the morning following a King Luncheon and birth date of Martin Luther King, Jr.

- To view the many organizations, bar associations, and political and humanitarian endeavors Dick further participated in, see the attached Addendum.

How does one soar to so many heights in life and then deal with discovering that now what confronts him seems bigger than life? Dick's faith became more prominent than ever. Can your faith ever be *big* enough?

How does one walk such a journey with their mate when they too realize the undeniable magnitude of such a situation? Not only did my faith expand, but I decided that when making a decision, whether it be one of immediate consequence or one of just moving through the day, to do so in a manner that I would have no regrets. It meant asking myself endless questions throughout those six years, but this practice will always be a part of my life. It is the determinant that gave and will continue to give me peace.

This might be a good place to mention that halfway through this journey, I became painfully aware of my own frailties and decided I should seek someone to help me along the way. I discovered the perfect counselor, who said she would never forget my very first words to her as I sat down in her office. They were, "I need your help, and I also need you to know that divorce is not an option." This statement was augmented by several things other than my vows upon marriage, which directed my footsteps. Having experienced divorce in my past, I was not going there again and certainly not because the going got tough. Plus, I felt a compassion for my husband that was profound.

I know that the Lord brings different people into our lives at different times, and I am adding "at the right time"…sometimes for a moment, or a day, or a season…even a lifetime. My counselor has been another source of strength in troubled times. Not all counselors are equal, and I was granted the best. Remember, it takes strength to recognize when help is needed, *and* it takes a receptive mind to benefit from that which is offered.

Thus the trek continued-

Dick fought injustice far and near. Neighborhood people could walk in off the street and get "Lawyer Roger's" attention just for the asking. His faith in God enabled him to practice law exactly as he thought it should be practiced. In representation of clients, he likened some of his battles to David versus Goliath, feeling he escaped adversity only by the grace of God.

Dick was known for his contributions and efforts beyond anything he/we ever knew. When I sold his office, I was surprised by a letter from a potential buyer, who was soon to become the awarded purchaser. Two offers prevailed. One from a community landlord and the other from a young and aspiring attorney out of a neighboring town who actually wrote how he hoped to pick up the baton that Dick carried for years in serving his neighborhood community and expand upon the journey. He knew of Dick but had never met him. Here was a young attorney so impressed by the life of another attorney who he had only heard of that it affected the course he was taking. Is it any wonder that the latter was awarded the purchase of this special emotional landmark? For me, the decision-maker, there was no contest.

Dick was so recognized and loved that some townspeople came in the office after his demise and asked if they could hug me—*me*—in remembrance of *D*. That took me only a moment to figure out. During the course of our marriage, I had come to recognize a kind of safety net around me. Those townspeople who revered "Lawyer Rogers," as they referred to him, saw me as an extension. They were motivated to protect me as well. It was amazing the sense of security that gave me, almost to the point of what one might see as foolhardy, but above all, I knew God prevailed in my life.

One might ask how it felt to be viewed as an extension of another. While I understood fully the need for individuality (having been raised an identical twin made that fact very clear to me early on), I was in no way threatened by the connection that was being made. Another lesson: If you have confidence in who you are, another's actions or thoughts cannot take that away from you. In fact, if you allow yourself to understand the intent, in some cases you may be quite a benefactor.

In this instance I was truly a benefactor as the area where Dick's office was situated was not safe at night and there were many nights, late, late into the night, that I would be there picking him up when he was unable to drive and be sternly directed not to get out of my car. Norristown was a town of active law offices by day, being that the courthouse was in the center of town. But by night, those doors were closed, locked tight…well, most of those doors, except for Dick's. He had a reputation for doing mega amounts of research in his second-floor library into the wee hours of the morning. I'm here to tell you that I lived that too. One might ask why I was willing to take him back and forth at such uncivilized hours, and I guess the best way to answer that is to say that I recognized the need of one I felt a compassion for and I was celebrating my wholeness, being grateful it was not me in such a circumstance.

And I was Dick's mate, his lifetime partner, committed to the journey wherever it should lead. My work career had to this point proven to be quite varied, starting out as a therapist in children services in Baltimore and reaching far into the telecommunications arena, interior decorating, marketing, and a number of unusual and exciting entrepreneurial endeavors. What I had learned was that God had granted me more than my share of unique gifts, some of which would be exhibited as my life ensued.

However, now my attentions were needed on the home front and my career came to an unplanned halt. As I proceed, you will become aware, as I did, of God's perfect timing.

And So It Began

There Is Always a Beginning

The year was 2000.

The season was summer.

The day was Saturday.

The time was 12:00 noon, six years before that day in mid-May 2006, when D asked me to come sit down on the bed next to him and took my hand in his.

Where? The place I called home (Connecticut) while growing up; soon to become an area I felt like I should avoid—I don't know about at all costs, but certainly with some trepidation.

The journey had just begun. What became immensely clear to me was that at any given moment, our lives can change dramatically. Actually, I already knew that, but I realized we are not necessarily limited to one such happening.

It was a hot summer day when we headed for Connecticut with great expectation of celebrating D's aunt's hundredth birthday. It is not uncommon for one to reach the centurion mark today, but as recent as ten years ago, it was viewed as extraordinarily remarkable, certainly a year to be well celebrated.

When we arrived at what we thought was our destination to greet those setting up for the big event, the church parking lot was empty. That meant scouting around. D started across the grassy island and, stepping off a curb, took quite a fall. Due to spinal complications, he was often unable to use his arms or hands to block a fall. Falls were something D was used to, if that is possible. He would rebound quickly, and most times, he rejected any help in the process of regaining his ground.

As I helped him up and found a shady area for him to sit and regroup, I noticed he lacked the energy that he normally exhibited when rebounding from these all-too-often tumbles. Within moments it was determined that he needed medical attention. He had bitten his lip so deeply that the bleeding did not start instantly.

After being directed to Bridgeport Hospital, D had some serious stitches put in his lip and was sent back to the hotel (which we still had not checked into), seemingly none the worse for what had just happened and feeling ready to give our trip the special attention that was intended. We were both relieved that quality care was found and we could move on.

Dinner with other family members who were present for the big event was a pleasant catch-up time, as it didn't happen often that we all got together. Birthdays, weddings, or funerals were the earmarks for reunion. After eating and all seeming well, we made our ways back to our rooms in anticipation of the forthcoming event the following day. How often does a 100th birthday happen, and in your own family? The idea of celebrating was foremost on our agendas.

At 5:30 in the morning, I was awakened to my husband's convulsing body. I didn't have any idea what was happening. As much as I had professed to know about the medical field, this happening totally eluded and frightened me. I grabbed D's shoulder and called his name, trying to stop him from shaking. No response. I tried again ... still no response ... and once more ... still no response. It was like his body was involuntarily rising off the bed and back and shaking violently at the same time. I was enveloped by a fear that once he stopped shaking, he would be gone— gone from this life.

With heart and feet both racing, I opened the door, calling to my brother-in-law, a doctor, who was in the room across the hall. It couldn't have been better planned and was not intentional. My belief that there are no mistakes was once again confirmed in my mind.

Lem heard my panicked calls. I was afraid to go knock on his door, knowing if I let go of my door, I wouldn't be able to get back in the room as nothing was at hand to hold the door back from closing. Where were these rational thoughts coming from when fear was so prevalent, front and center? Again, I say the Lord was right there with me. How grateful I was that Lem heard and came over, only to discover D having a very serious grand mal seizure.

The summoned ambulance was there in minutes, taking D back to the Bridgeport Hospital. As we were waiting for him to be evaluated, I made a quick call to my minister's home to ask for prayer. I came to realize the power of prayer in years prior. There were not exceptions.

In the hospital just an hour later, while doing a CAT scan to determine the cause, D suffered another seizure that all but took his life. We were told to call the children and have them come up from Pennsylvania. After two days in ICU, not knowing much, he started showing signs of the man I knew, who now knew me.

My brother-in-law stayed longer than planned to make certain all was on the right track before leaving to go home. I was grateful. At one point, I remember Lem suggesting I go back to the hotel to get some much-needed sleep, but I felt concerned that D would gain awareness and be looking for a familiar face. I could not leave. I had learned earlier in my life that I needed to listen to my heart even if someone was giving me directions that made sense. I was remaining true to my heart. This was another one of those "don't live to regret" moments.

We were in Bridgeport Hospital for one and a half weeks. I was able to find a room some miles away, as I had been seriously instructed that the surrounding areas were not safe. My sweet niece, Cher, who happened to live in a neighboring town, brought me clothing to wear as I only had packed two changes, not knowing that our visit would be prolonged.

Through all of this, it was unequivocally apparent that God was there, taking care of each thing we needed each step of the way. The amazing thing is that many times when trauma occurs, you don't even know what it is you need at a given moment, but as you move through the event, you realize what has been directed your way without your ever even asking. Does it get much better than that?

After this experience, D and I came to feel that the state of Connecticut was an omen for us. In 1994 I suffered a major subarachnoid hemorrhage (an aneurysm thought to have come from a fall I had taken in a grocery store eight years earlier) upon arriving in Connecticut for a family get-together. After two weeks in the Norwalk Hospital literally fighting for life, I returned home to a number of month's recuperation and a life of gratitude that the Lord had blessed me to live on, when most having such an episode don't. Those who do are more than likely disabled. I was spared and have been forever grateful.

Here are the similarities. Imagine the following: Two people (spouses), two trips to Connecticut for family events, two happenings requiring immediate hospitalization, two head injuries, two experiences of memory loss, two ICU situations, two over one-week hospital stays, two near-death episodes. Connecticut did not beacon to us after this. In fact, not even being superstitious, we still had reserve about wanting to travel north.

Thus, our rocky road had begun-

Periodic seizures became a course of events for D. I could always tell when they were impending, usually in the early-morning hours, and I also knew there was no stopping them. There was little relief from the anxiety that I felt in watching this take place. On one level, I would want to sleep lightly to help, not giving any conscious thought to the fact that there was no way I would be able to sleep through such an event anyway. On occasion, I would wonder that perhaps if I noticed one coming in the slightest way, maybe, just maybe, I could change the course and prevent the happening; *is* that not grandiose? On another level, I longed for nights of deeper sleep as total rest was rather scarce.

I had been advised because of the magnitude of D's seizures that he should be taken to the hospital each time. The local police and ambulance staff were getting to know us. There were no longer questions as to where he was, or which way was the right room. First the police and then the ambulance crew knew exactly where to go and always found a limp, unresponsive body awaiting care, totally exhausted from the convulsing event.

As much as I feared that D would have seizures while in activity, where he would be more likely to incur injury, I can only remember two times that he was not sleeping when this happened.

For those who have not dealt with seizures, they bring with them a major restriction for one who is independent, which is not being able to drive for six months, assuming no further seizures. Imagine how one would feel after waiting five and a half months to have another seizure just before the six months is up. For D, this was a fate almost as bad as the physical ones presenting themselves on a daily basis. For one who is extremely independent, you don't want another to have to take you every place you want to, or have to, go. Thus, a major frustration ensued. Somehow, my pointing out that he might perceive himself as fortunate to have someone who was able and happy to meet his time requirements and desires as to when he wanted to be somewhere did not seem to make his disappointment less burdensome.

As D was doctoring for the seizures, unable to drive and unsettled about his need to be taken any and everywhere he wanted or needed to go, he continued to move forward almost like nothing had happened. Sometimes I felt like he was in a trance, and maybe he was, and one might add, understandably.

Once D finally regained his license after the six-month waiting period, he was back behind the wheel only two times. Very shortly thereafter, another seizure would appear. How discouraging! Knowing him as I did, I would feel very confident in saying it wasn't the actual seizure that disturbed D nearly as much as having his license confiscated one more time.

It was difficult knowing that his safety and the safety of others appeared to be in jeopardy if he should get his license back, for at this point, the risk of seizures was not the only issue. His reflex time due to his compromised mobility weighed heavily in the picture. Here I was, praying against his one desire and hope that he hung on to: *autonomy*. We had become opposing forces.

There were a couple times when I thought I was going to have to take unwanted possession of the car keys, when better judgment was not in focus, when the desire to defy all the rules prevailed, when it was drive/do or die, and when reasoning as to the risk for self and others on the road had little meaning. I must add here, not intentionally.

It was extremely difficult to watch a vibrant, determined, persevering man lose control of the few things left that equated to a degree of independence.

My belief that within each adversity there are positives kept me focused on the silver linings within each cloud. There were so many clouds that you would have thought our lives would be shimmering with beauty. Actually, there was beauty in the form of hope—hope that prevailed amidst the pain.

The Falls of a Proud Man

Pride that Standeth in the Way

The falls countless, most injuries untold, pride battered; but the walk, the compromised gait, the winter spasms, continued—continued for over six years.

The following speaks to only moments and particular events—a major broad-brush of this aspect of our lives. You might wonder why I say "our" lives. Anyone who has a child can more than likely relate when I say that when one you care about gets hurt, be it physically or emotionally, do you not hurt as well? I believe you would. Can you not be a part of the pain? I wouldn't know how.

One late August evening in 2005, D had asked me to take him to the office; there was something he needed to pick up. As we approached his building he reminded me, as he always did, not to get out of the car. "Stay in the car," his voice echoed. By night, the area around the office became much less safe than it was by daylight, and even then, there was reason for a degree of caution. I always assessed my surroundings as I transitioned from car to office, day or night. Actually, I am not certain I felt much safer waiting in the car, but at moments like this, I guess you take the less risky route, and that is a matter of one's interpretation. However, try to reason in opposition with a trial attorney... My only comment would be, "*Good luck.*" D had previously explained, if I walked into the office with him, he would have to worry about two of us. While I understood what he was saying, I also understood clearly what I was feeling.

As I was waiting for him to come back, I was aware of the minutes ticking away, ticking away, ticking away. Anxiety was setting in, for too many minutes had ticked away. Then I saw him walk past a window and assured myself that all was fine. The minutes started ticking away again; only this time, there were too many minutes. Those minutes, by now, had turned into segments that almost equaled an hour. All of a sudden, I noticed the leaves on a plant near the door moving as if in a breeze.

D's office was a century-old funeral home turned into offices. The front entrance had double French doors and square windowpanes from top to almost bottom with matching side panels. Most of the panes were frosted, but a few strategically placed ones were made of clear glass. In retrospect, maybe those in clear glass were placed by happenstance. As you walked through these doors, you were instantly in a foyer with a secretary's suite off to each side before entering the waiting room.

It was into one of those secretarial offices that I saw D walk. It was through one of the clear panes that I saw those leaves swaying. It was a hot evening, but I knew there was no central air or a fan in the area to be propelling a breeze. Questions and more questions started to flood my mind. Then I saw something bobbing up and down at the bottom window, a frosted pane. Questions and more questions … *What on earth could that be?*

I wanted to jump out of the car and check what was happening, but I was mentally reminded that I needed to stay in the car. When I realized that what I saw bobbing up and down was D, it no longer mattered that he did not want me to exit the car. When I got to the door with no key—he always locked the door behind himself for safety—I saw, through one of only three clear glass panes, he had fallen and had managed to get himself to the door to try to get my attention. Talking through the mail slot, with my direction and the little fortitude he had left, we were able to get him to his feet. When I suggested getting help, which I did in rare instances, it *never* seemed to be an option, but I must gratefully say *almost always* we managed the necessary maneuvers to bring D to a standing position.

If he had been seriously injured in a fall, there would have been no options. However, I always tried to give as much leeway as possible for success within our private realm. It was important for D to have some sense of autonomy within his steadily declining situation. I felt that gave extra endurance to the strength he was continually trying to muster. I knew unequivocally at that period of time that he was still fighting to "stand tall" with every fiber he possessed.

I learned if I told D that I was going to call for help, somehow an extra ingredient got added to the mix to bring a desired result. As much as I had come to understand this, I only did that as a very last resort, when I really believed help was needed, which was the only way he or I would have wanted it.

While pride can stand in the way of many things and be viewed as a negative, such as in the case of being vain, I also know that there is a *positive* side to *pride*. I would call that the recognition of self-sufficiency.

However, this particular evening I saw an obstacle that neither D nor I could do anything about immediately—a locked door. I suggested getting the police to come and help, but got a resounding, "*No.*" I immediately became grateful for the large, heavy planter next to the door that, in this instance, became his anchor and aid. Thus, D was once again up and ready to "carry on."

Trips to the office were always emotionally troublesome for me. D would often want to work into the early-morning hours by himself, even when his practice started slowing down. Having the opportunity to do research in his library, on the second floor, was like frosting on a cake for him.

Whether a case was imminent or not, there was still an allurement that beaconed and did not allow for a naysayer.

However, this naysayer was very concerned about D going up and down steps when alone. D would start down the stairs and upon each step, his momentum would build. It was always at a running pace that kept him moving well beyond the point of reaching the last step due to his building speed. God was always present, pulling him back and receiving quick little prayers from me.

They should have been off limits—off limits, because there was no hope for a gentleman's agreement to staying on the first floor. Giving up the steps that led to his library/sanctuary was not something that a very proud man with unusual determination and perseverance was willing to acquiesce to.

The falls continued-

One evening in early 2006, I heard this noise from the master bathroom. I suspected a fall. As I walked through the bedroom, I saw the door to the master bathroom closed and I called to D. There was no answer. I called again … no answer. I tried to open the door. It seemed locked. I was sure it wasn't locked, as that would have been a first. I called again, saying, "Dick, I need to know that you are okay."

He quietly, almost inaudibly, said, "Fine." Just one word, "*fine*." Did his "fine" mean, "That's fine that you need to know," *or* "Yes, I am fine"? While I don't believe in stereotyping, I did discover the uniqueness of communicating with someone in the field of law.

Well, I knew he wasn't fine and figured he had fallen in a way that his body was against the door, preventing me from opening it. Communication was close to nil—not totally uncommon since the onset of Alzheimer's. Finally, I was able to convince him to move just enough to allow me to open the door so I could help. Once the door was open, he was able to slide his body into the bedroom and use certain pieces of furniture for leverage, and voila!—once again a standing position. Somehow, there would always be a sense of accomplishment and gratefulness each time we returned to our "normal."

When I went back into the bathroom that evening, I saw a dent in the wall where he had hit his head in the fall. In talking with the doctor at that time, I discovered that a hematoma in the brain from falls often does not show up immediately. At a later point, I was rather shocked to discover that D had a number of hematomas.

As the falls continued my suggestion of a walker for additional support was given little credence, if any. I knew D viewed that as acquiescing long before he needed to. I felt fortunate that he was willing to use a cane, which came about with great duress. To be sure, each cane he owned, and there were a few, was chosen with great discernment. They were in no way your traditional cane. In fact, we seldom went anywhere that someone would not stop and ask him about his cane.

There was one time, only one, before the last year of disability that D acquiesced to a wheel chair. As you might imagine, the event for which it was needed had to be of utmost importance—his brother Peter's swearing in as a judge in Philadelphia, Pennsylvania.

By 2004 and thereafter, when I was working, I always made it a point to go home at lunch time and see what was needed other than making lunch, for it was often at this point of the day that D would want me to take him into his office. There would be a bit to accomplish in an hour's lunch period. I would have moments of frustration, wanting to please his desire to go to the office, but not wanting to be late going back to my office. So I would try to encourage him to be ready to go before I arrived home, but I believed deep in my heart because of his Alzheimer's, reasoning took a whole different perspective.

Actually, I am not sure that "reasoning" was any longer a word with any significance in our vocabulary. I needed it, but it just was not there. Talk about looking for strength in difficult moments... I *prayed* for a way to compensate that would bring me a sense of peace. I never was able to find a substitute process, but I just kept moving through and making the best of what was, knowing that *this too shall pass*. "This is only a moment in time," I would tell myself.

It was amazing the reassurance those very words gave me. *This is only a moment in time.* I'm here to tell you today that that is all it was.

Perhaps that was the answer to my prayer—the realization that *this is only a moment in time.* We had many such moments yet to endure.

On one of those days he did not go into the office, at about 4:00 p.m., I received a call from our alarm service company saying that Dick had called for help and the police could not get into the house. Of course, I hurried home. We found D on the floor in the bedroom, face down and unable to turn his head. It appeared he may have been lying there for a while. I forget now how that was determined, but as I remember, it appeared to have been at least two hours. It hurt me to see him with his face forward in the carpet, unable to turn his head for relief. I could feel the tears welling with no place to go. It started at a gut level and just stayed there. This was a feeling I was all too familiar with, and it would continue to visit me as D's illnesses progressed. There were times for crying and times for being strong. While I don't believe crying or lack of crying defines strength, it can impact the moment at hand. In D's decline, I felt the need for strength/peace to prevail.

D wore an alarm, watchband style, but had not used it right away. Looking back, I don't know whether he forgot he had that capability, whether he was determined to get up on his own, or whether he was waiting for me to arrive home naturally. I guess there are other possibilities, but what really mattered was the state he was in for a period of time, gratefully with no apparent physical injury.

What I came to realize was that the alarm system that gave me some sense of peace was not the total answer. Then again, was anything? I was not inclined to want to get that philosophical, not then and there...actually, not even now. It was the best we had for the moment. Actually, that was the only time he ever used it.

I ask myself if D may have had a greater sense of peace if he could have felt in his soul that standing tall does not have to mean feet on the ground!

Life's Necessary Changes

Compelling Choices

Do we always have a choice, even if it is to do nothing? There have been times when I have said there was no choice, but actually, there was, just not a good one or one that seemed like a lateral move. Of course, we always hope that any choice we make will not worsen the circumstance.

Oftentimes, people will say, "God has not answered my prayer," when in fact, the answer can be in the absence of an answer or in having to wait for an action. As I learned during these long six years, God's timing is perfect, regardless of what I would think I needed at a given moment. My moment was not the perfect moment, and at those times, there always proved to be a reason for the waiting.

Choices and timing go hand in hand.

Move and move and move, we did-

When D and I married, we lived in a wonderful, old farm home on a beautiful property. This home had a center hall that went from the front door to the back door. Off the hall to the left through French doors were a dining room, sunroom, and kitchen. Off to the right through another set of French doors was a large living room. Once in the living room, there was a set of French doors on either side of a fireplace leading to an outside veranda. Upstairs were three large bedrooms and a full bath, and on the third floor, two more bedrooms and full bath. Throughout there were touches of quaintness that spoke to our decorating fancies.

When the stairs became a daily challenge for D, we knew we needed to consider one-floor living. This in no way would be a happy decision, for D revered his farm home, which he had gotten years before he "got me." The home was surrounded by lovely grounds, flat with grass groomed like velvet carpet. The wedding of Tracey, D's daughter, was held under a tent in the backyard. It was beautifully perfect.

Now, I must admit there was a slight draw back to this charming farm for a suburbia girl like me. Our farm home was like living on a reserve. The natural habitat brought about many creatures: fox, deer, possums, badgers, raccoon, skunks, and mice, and I am certain I have missed a few. It was unsettling to come home in the evening; park in our garage, which was situated at least twenty-five yards from the house; and see eyes shining in the dark, leaving a high degree of uncertainty as to which specific creature they belonged. Or how about a badger crossing a tree limb above your head? I was told that was impossible, but my stepson, Richard, bore credence to the fact after seeing a like event. I never followed that same path to or from the garage again without scanning Mother Nature carefully and moving quickly, for I knew that if a badger lost footing and fell on me, that fat, furry fellow would certainly bring me close to a heart attack.

Despite my fearful uncertainty as to what might greet me any given evening, and considering all the wonderful and lovely aspects of our home, it was clear the day would come, or so we thought, that the steps would be insurmountable. We preferred to make a move of our own volition and not out of dire need, which would limit our choices. As it was, we looked for quite a few months in a start-and-stop pattern.

Yes, we had a choice, but life's circumstances were causing us to consider options that would drastically affect our existence based on our decision. "Sensibility" is perhaps the word here. What makes the most sense regardless of the limitations?

Our initial goal to find a ranch home was to no avail. Finally, we found a condo that D said he could see himself coming home to. It had a prime position within a small community setting—just perfect as condos go. We told ourselves it was as close as you could get to owning a single home within a shared-complex living.

Moving from a single home in a beautiful setting that epitomized your dream and that, in part, motivated the energy that propelled your career, can be very difficult to do.

How many times, as we approach our later years or are experiencing declining health, do we say, "This is not what was in the plan, not the way I would have ever expected it to be." It can make us feel as if our choices are limited to none, though there may be feasible options.

So in a winter in the very late nineties we gave up our wonderful farm home because of the stairs. There was an *irony*, however, a huge, "is this for real" kind of irony. D never gave up steps totally, especially the ones leading to his library and research in his office.

Some things were just not going to happen. The same risk presented itself at the office as at home, but you do learn when an issue is not within your control, in spite of expressed logic. There just was no hope for reasoning. There is that word again, "reasoning." What I did discover was that in each of these situations where I prayed for reasoning, it would eventually play itself out—given enough time. *Time is a wonderful thing.* Sounds familiar, doesn't it? The message is to be patient. Patience will bring peace.

When I was young, time almost always moved too slowly. As I have gotten older, time often moves too fast. *And* yet, this thing called time, this period of life that speaks to all that has been and all that will be, keeps moving, and in the process, issues are remarkably resolved.

My solace was in knowing that this day would come and this day would go. *Regardless*, with the passage of each day would be the hope for a brighter tomorrow or an issue resolved or greater insight, whatever was needed. Sometimes we think we know what is needed. I learned we may not always have that answer. There may be something awaiting us far greater than we would have dared to hope for.

Through my journey, I truly learned the importance of patience. I always thought I was patient, but I am talking about *real patience*: knowing that by sitting back and not second guessing or trying to make something happen or to make something different, that what needs to happen will happen.

Back to the stairs and our compelling choices-

Actually, our move to High Gate did not totally eliminate steps either, for even though all the amenities needed, including the master bedroom suite, were on the first floor, there was a now-and-then attraction to venture to the second floor, which housed a guest bedroom, a sitting room, and a double bath.

I remember holding my breath at times when D would use the powder room on the landing leading to the second floor, for even though it was just one step up, it presented some challenges.

Sometimes I would be convinced that he was testing his abilities or perhaps just did not calculate the risk ratio. Why take a risk when everything was available to you that spelled s-a-f-e? That was my question. Oh, I can surmise, but we cannot assume what another is thinking, so I just kept calling on God to walk with us. D had a poignant little book called *Walking with the Shepherd* that he carried everywhere. This book gave a detailed translation of the Twenty-third Psalm. It never seemed to be more than an arm's reach away.

In 2005, what seemed like out of the clear blue, D suggested I look for a smaller place for us to move to. Our expenses had become rather high, and we did not need the amount of space we had. Later I realized there was something else motivating his suggestion. He urged me to look for a home in the fifty-five-plus community where my sister and mother shared a home. Was it that he liked what he saw that much when we visited them? Somehow, I didn't think that was the answer, despite the fact that they had a lovely home. However, it was the kind of request as he posed it that caused me to respond without having to delve into the whys.

At first, he would not join me in looking. When I found a place and asked him to look at it with me, he declined until I convinced him that this was not a move that I was making alone and that his acceptance of the home was just as important as mine. There could be no other way from my vantage point, as long as he was able.

I had found a place one-half the size of what we were then living in, but guess what—*no stairs* and only one step going out the front door to the car. That was definitely doable. Looking back, I believe it was the only home available at that time in that particular community. Was it just waiting for us? Being one who believes all things happen with reason, I did not need to see anything else, under the circumstances, since this would meet our needs as pleasantly as possible.

D did agree to join me in looking and deciding, but it was obvious his heart was not really there, except to be sure I felt I could be comfortable there. I'm not certain my heart was in it, either. In fact, I will say it was not. I was going through the motions of house hunting, knowing in my heart it was one of the choices that was the best under the circumstances and knowing I'd do whatever was necessary to make such a change as positive as possible. Feeling that tug in my gut that all but led to tears.

And so it was, our last home together was purchased, with D knowing that it was more than likely he would leave this world before me. And so he did.

The Agony of Alzheimer's

Before Reality Diminishes

One sunny Saturday in late April 2000, with me as the designated driver, D and I were on our way to the Penn Relays, a never-missed event; for D it was almost as important as the air he breathed. Approaching the general area, I asked him for directions. Previously as a passenger, it was something I never paid much attention to and was curiously surprised and very interested when he said he didn't know where we were or which street to turn on. I found our way and moved on through the day. In the back of my mind, I couldn't let go of what I had experienced just hours before.

It was soon brought to D's neurologist's attention that D was forgetting things he had been aware of for decades. In the process, after careful evaluation, he was given one of the Alzheimer's medications without an actual diagnosis, but rather it was just something to help with the forgetfulness. I would never have questioned the doctor in front of D as to what was suspected, for I saw that as *his* question when *he* was ready to hear the answer. If I needed an answer, I would have to do that on my own time, if I could even get the information with the HIPA regulations being what they are. I also viewed it as a label that would not change the course of events. There was no reason to push to hear that dreadful word, not for me and I know *not for D*.

I believed that in not hearing a label there was less emphasis on each action that might have otherwise seemed more alarming. From my vantage point, the only reason for a label was to make certain you were aware of any old/new medical or natural approaches in treating the particular condition. You want to know you have searched all the possibilities and given each an appropriate degree of consideration. We are consumers even in the medical field.

When put through the series of questions by his neurologist in testing his memory, D always was right on top of the situation. No reason for that to be any different; that was his style. His doctor later explained that one who is very intelligent and extremely well read will more than likely manifest the symptoms of Alzheimer's differently.

D read two to three newspapers every day, not to mention the amount of literature he consumed in research for his law practice. He was noted for the amount of research he did. Plus, he would often sit up through the whole night reading a chosen novel. D used to tell of sitting on the top of a straight-back dining-room chair to study in college, to prevent falling asleep. That is discipline; I know had it been me, I'd have succumbed to my tiredness and found myself sprawled on the floor. Those who know me might chuckle at the thought that there might have been a chance I would have slept right through the experience.

After many months of taking the Alzheimer's medication Aricept, D had another Alzheimer's medication, Namenda, added to the mix. One day while waiting to see the neurologist, we each, unaware of the other's action, picked up some corresponding literature in the doctor's office. We felt certain, after reading it, of what we were now facing without having been spoken to. Actually, we thought we knew all along, but we didn't allow it to absorb into our minds. Now what we believed to be the facts had edged their way into consciousness.

When we arrived home that day in 2005, D sat in his lift chair in the family room. You could have almost equated his lift chair to a teddy bear—it was a great comfort zone. I sat in an adjacent loveseat. After moments of silence, I looked over at D. I will never forget the look I saw in his eyes when we dared to use the word *Alzheimer's*: the fear, how this intelligent, in-charge attorney could possibly be facing such a fate; the reconciliation for the suspicion that had been there for some time; the pain, omnipresent. Hadn't enough already attacked his physical being? I longed to relieve his spirit of this unknown venture he/we were about to embark on, knowing that it would be oh, so agonizing.

Appealing to D's intelligence and looking for purpose through what we knew would be troubled times, I suggested we start a journal and keep a record of events to possibly help others that would follow in a similar path, a journal that would give others ideas on how to compensate, to rise as high as possible above each day's happenings. D would understand the benefit of helping others. His was the only law practice where anyone from the neighborhood could walk in off the street and ask for his time. He always gave of his services generously, time allowing, with no thought of remuneration. As you might imagine, the boundaries of the neighborhood grew and grew.

My idea about the journal, however, was quietly vetoed. An affirmative response never came, nor the willingness to participate, so that idea was promptly put to rest. After all, this was his illness; he needed to embrace it in whatever way was tolerable for him. As to this journey, I was his helpmate, there to make the walk as tolerable as possible.

D and I, in our church work as a deacon/deaconess, had already experienced the regression of a number of our fellow congregants suffering memory loss during our regular visits to countless nursing homes, which at times were quite heart wrenching. I remember the day I approached our deacons and suggested that D needed relief from the task of going out and giving communion, a service in which I always accompanied him. It finally became a struggle that I'm not even certain he was totally cognizant of. Maybe part of the blessing, at times, is that you don't know you don't know. However, that can only be a speculation from an observer, for how can we ever really know what another is thinking if they are unable to express it to us? Even when they can express it, it is left to interpretation. At any rate, I was definitely observing the challenge and the need for relief. While D did not verbally agree that it was time to be relieved of this task, he did not mind my relaying such a message. Now, that was unusual and totally out of character. In my heart I felt he did recognize that a change was needed, one that he himself would have never spoken to.

One day, well into his treatment for Alzheimer's, I was doing laundry as D was starting to cook. I was beginning to discourage this activity mainly for safety reasons. I noticed, as I looked into the kitchen area, a frying pan smoking, probably close to flames, and there was D standing right next to it, chopping vegetables as if nothing around him was amiss. As I hurried over to the stove, I called to D, afraid that any given moment the smoking frying pan would be ablaze. There was no response. I knew then we needed to relegate D to using just a crock-pot.

I did not want him to not be able to cook if he so desired. Lima bean soup and cherry pie were his favorites. I don't believe I ever saw so much work and love go into a cherry pie. Can a cherry pie be over loved? Oh, believe me, it can. When one takes well over an hour to create a cherry pie you can imagine the concentrated effort that is attached to each detail. I felt like I should be helping, but that would have compromised the intricacy of D's creation. There was something slightly endearing and humorous in observing the process.

Amidst the trauma, one still needs to find the humor. I remember when I was a young therapist working in the psych field at a catchment area in Baltimore City. New in the field and to the staff, I was a little taken back by the staff laughing at some situations that didn't seem very funny to me. I realize there are times in life when you must look for the humor and that it is okay as long as it is not at another's expense. It can be the humor that keeps you sane in a situation that makes no sense.

To think the challenges ended with a brand new crock-pot presented on our kitchen counter would be a gross understatement—or maybe it was an overstatement. D felt that yet another act of independence had been whisked away from him, and he was right. As much as I felt his pain, I had a responsibility to our safety and that of our neighbors with adjoining homes. However, compliance was not one of D's traits, so the crock-pot was short lived.

All this brought about a strong desire for a great set of carving knives to ready the vegetables for that lima bean soup. The existing ones would no longer fit the bill. For me—more concern, more prayers.

Very early in 2006, D's cooking was fast becoming an opposition for us. We were entering into a period that remained where nothing tasted right—*nothing*!—and a period of feeling I was an adversary. When one is quickly losing their autonomy, how do you convince them of your devotion to what is best for them, that you would love to diminish their pain, when, in fact, they see you as causing it? What I knew was that I wanted to remain strong, loving, and not take the expressed disenchantment personally, knowing in my heart it was intended for the situation. One way I dealt with this was to ask the doctor to share with D what he felt he needed to know, and then D and I could address the situation, hopefully with a sense of unity based on the doctor's input. This did not work most of the time, for Alzheimer's did not allow for that type of reasoning. There is that word again!

On to nothing tasting right-

Believe me, this was traumatic for a man who approached eating like an adventure. If he didn't have time to sit and enjoy a meal, D did not eat. Plus, I always mused that he had a style of eating, where even things I truly couldn't get past my mind block, like pig feet, looked good. *And*, if you liked what he was eating, you would have to indulge before it was over.

I remember a one-month period where each time I would pick D up at his office, as we were approaching home, he would tell me he wanted to go to a particular restaurant, each time a new one. It became a little disconcerting as many would be rather upscale, and at that particular time, finances where compromised by medical/medicine costs. We trudged on, day in and day out looking for the perfect meal. My question was, *What would it look like?* I came to realize—it did not exist.

In my efforts to please, one evening when we made it home to have dinner, I prepared one of D's favorites: baby lamb chops, mashed potatoes with gravy (never enough gravy), greens, sautéed peppers, and rolls with butter—a must. I remember the hope and excitement in my heart as I served him his dinner. At that point, he almost always ate dinner from a tray while sitting on his lift chair, watching television. One does not look for formality when you realize just a light heart would make your day.

I was walking back to the kitchen to get my dinner to join him when I heard footsteps behind me. As I looked around, I saw D following me with his dinner plate in hand, delivering it to the counter, not the least bit interested in its appealingly arranged content. Oh my, frustration was welling up. Where next? What to try next? In desperation, I called my wonderful stepchildren for input as to what their dad might like. We decided on some traditional soul food.

Actually, I had become a fairly good soul food chef in my efforts to please over the years, which meant cooking two different dinners each evening because of the variations in our eating styles—mine being somewhat vegetarian. But now we put my skills on the backburner and called on old friends, all to no avail. I guess the taste buds had retired and eating was now nothing more than a texture experience, if even that—another loss for D.

I was ready to try anything. D felt like I wasn't checking with him about what would taste good. He wouldn't know what to suggest, and anything I suggested was out of question or not worthy of comment. I recognized, once again, our opposing forces—my desire to satisfy and his need to maintain or recreate his revered eating experiences.

As imaginative as I liked to think I was, there didn't seem to be a palatable answer. If there was, I never found it.

This period, in late 2005 and early 2006, lent to other happenings as well.

I was becoming a mind reader. It was getting to where D just functioned with motion as opposed to comment or discussion. I would see him getting ready to go out, with no comment. The finishing touch would be his hat as he headed for the door. Almost always, at this point, the destination was his office. If I asked where he wanted to go, there would be no response. Somehow our lives were becoming a dance without music; however, the sync was amazing.

In this disabling process, I saw a change in D's temperament. For example, one day at the bank he was quite indignant at being asked to show his license. I could see the traces of his background, that of a lawyer in the foreground. Not certain where the heated discussion was going to lead, I dropped behind him and indicated to the teller to let it be. D caught my cautioning motion and immediately questioned my taking sides and I understood that, but resolve came quickly.

I found that the area of finances was fast becoming mine to handle in total when he asked for help one day in adding some figures. This was after hours, and I mean hours, of laboring over a rather simple issue. I watched the experience unfold. D's asking for help in this area was monumental. I couldn't help but wonder if he realized how long he struggled before asking.

Not that it mattered.

D's last day in court-

One day, in a very roundabout way, D asked me to drive him and to go into the courthouse and the courtroom with him for a hearing, not a trial. The invitation, more like a request to join him, came in stages. At this point, his gait was looking very compromised and his whole demeanor was lacking the confidence that D exuded whenever he entered a room or situation. I remember feeling so scared for him, not having any idea what the results could be if he was unable to carry this off. I also recognized at this moment that there was little I could do to support him, other than to offer physical aid, emotional encouragement, and prayer—prayer that was never ending.

As the case before his was winding down, my heart was beating faster and faster. How could I save him from what he was about to do? Did I need to? The moment came and he had to work his way forward with great challenge, with me carrying his files and materials to the table he would be using. When he was set up, I went back to a nearby seat in the courtroom, noticing with relief that the judge seemed to be giving D a sympathetic eye. *Please Lord*, I prayed, *let him get through this with dignity. Please*, I begged. *Please Lord.*

As the minutes unfolded, I felt my spirit cheering him on. Yes, yes—that was good. He maintained a presence that was remarkable under the circumstances. It reminded me of a rote skill that one has and never loses, for D had been in the courtroom countless times, having the reputation of a pretty darn good trial attorney—one you did not necessarily want to come up against. His lawyer logic was present in everyday situations as well. I am not certain what D felt as he walked away or if he even realized how well he carried on despite his hindrances, but I knew I was happy for him at that moment.

Carry on! How often I heard that statement from D's dad when I would visit him, which was quite regularly in the final months of his life. I never left without him saying, "Carry on." Carry on—those words gave me a feeling of someone rooting for you and I liked that. I bet D heard those words growing up, for he surely made it a lifestyle to carry on.

The Hope of Two
Major Surgeries

Does Hope Spring Eternal?

Prelude to Surgery

D's first cervical surgery occurred in the late seventies before I knew him, at which time he forfeited a special government appointment in Washington DC because of being on a five-point walker for a period of time. This had been a major disappointment.

The only other career disappointment I heard him ever mention was a decision he made not to accept a commission in the navy. On occasion, he would say that, in retrospect, that was something he wished he had done.

D had had a couple car accidents, one in 1969 and one in 1980, with injuries resulting in profound arthritis in his cervical spine. The Connecticut drama was most probably brought on by the unsteadiness he experienced in walking due to his cervical condition. His gait was compromised, especially so in the cold months when uncontrollable spasms would set in.

There would often be times of understandable denial, like the fall in Connecticut; we really had to study the curb for faults. Part of that investigation could have been precipitated by the "Attorney" in front of D's name. However, it was an ordinary curb with no flaws to be found.

Watching him negotiate the walking process often left me feeling slightly helpless, as I wanted to make it easier. That was the nurturing side of me that had to find solace in knowing he was much happier making it on his own. I really couldn't make it better. *Imagine that.* Isn't it amazing the credit we can give ourselves at times? How many times had I seen him fall and not accept help to come back to a standing position? How many times had I restrained from jumping into the event, thinking my assistance was the answer? However, there were times it *was* the answer. The test was in the knowing which times it was.

A time comes to mind when he got out of the car to start walking to the front door of our house as I pulled the car into its parking place; it was easier that way. I watched as he approached the door and then I continued to park. All of a sudden, I saw a flash in my peripheral vision. It was just that—a flash that went zooming by. I was shocked to realize it was D propelling down the sloped driveway in brisk motion. As he reached the street area, he went into running circles without being able to stop. I jumped out of the car to aid him in bringing the helpless motion to a halt. My heart ached.

To one who literally loves words and the dynamics they bring to our relationships, it is difficult for me to understand that there are times when there are *no* words that make any sense. Instead, just the outreach of a helping hand, a look that says, "I hurt with you," says it all. Can we even begin to understand what one is feeling during such moments of duress? I think we can only imagine. During this period of my life, I learned just how golden silence can be.

I was astounded to know that many things can be affected by the condition of your cervical spine, right down to breathing. Oh, I have heard of people falling and severing spinal cords, thus becoming totally disabled: tragic. Equally tragic is a disability that slowly, insidiously, progresses with no regard for its recipient—a disability that gradually removes control of the body's natural functions, diminishing any hope of recovery. In such instances, not only is one becoming gradually dependent and losing autonomy, but embracing life also becomes a challenge as it whittles away.

What amazed many was the tenacity and perseverance with which D continued through life. He had a faith that became remarkable as he moved forward with determined strength. I came to realize how I mirrored that level of tenacity and perseverance as I walked by his side, each step, each anguished step along our journey.

Did we gain additional strength from each other? I think, perhaps, we may have. I like that thought.

I believe life is a series of learning and teaching experiences. Certainly, and rather constantly at this juncture, both D and I were learning—learning how to face major challenges with fortitude and grace. Our faith was surely being tested. I always viewed our situation as a *challenge* rather than a *problem*. It isn't just semantics. I believed and do believe in seeing each situation through with determination, finding the positive within, and thanking the Lord for each blessing that every day brings.

Does strength come from faith? From a belief system fostered in formative years? From an experience in which innate abilities were realized? From the support of another being? I'm certain the list could go on and on.

While I don't know what motivates another's tenacity, I can speak as to myself. I was raised to believe that I am a survivor and to have courage of my convictions, which kept and keeps me encouraged to move beyond any hindrances. Both those aspects accompanied me down the many challenging paths I have encountered even long before D and I met and married. However, this six-year season of my life was the ultimate test.

Here is a silver lining! In being a survivor, I learned a number of skills. The one I relate to the most is problem solving, which, in turn, made me resourceful. Within my resourcefulness, I discovered many God-given gifts and skills that turned many minuses into pluses. I must put God into the equation, for He is my all and all. He is my source in troubled times, my source in joyful times, and I will thank Him always. He has equipped me with gifts and grace.

I feel totally confident that I am no exception. God is ever-present for each and every one of us. The best part is that He is right here, right now, *and* He is there right now. *Here* and *there* is *everywhere*. If called on, no matter when or where, God is always listening.

In the sales arena, there is a saying that for every no you receive, say thank you, because it brings you that much closer to a yes; it's in the numbers. Likewise, while we are challenged and troubled by the traumas that touch our lives, they do make us stronger and truly more appreciative of the happy times when they appear. It is not the trauma itself in our lives that gives us strength, it is the realization that we made it through. *What is it that gets you through?*

Or, if you are in the midst of such a journey, I urge you to trust in your faith.

I was forever expressing my gratitude, for I knew how easy it would be to crumble. I also knew that to crumble would not make things better, and I wanted to make each day the very best that it could be under the circumstances. Do those sound like words of a survivor? I thank the Lord for waking me up and for my health and sound mind to experience another day, each and every day.

During the last years of that six-year period, as I rode in my car, almost every day, I was fortifying my spirit with music of praise—praise that I had God in my life to lean on—and assuring myself that He was there for me, and would grant me the grace I needed to walk this walk. "I Sing Praises to Your Name, I Sing Praises to Your Name,

Oh Lord." I never missed a day of thanking God for His presence in our lives and for my well-being; for what was happening to D could have been happening to me, and I never lost sight of this. I was especially aware of my own vulnerabilities after having an aneurysm that left me fighting for my life in 1994.

I do not address God with the same fervency each day as I did during that six-year period. There are times when our endurance wanes—not our desires, not our direction—but just sheer energy. People find strength in emergent situations. Well, my situation lasted six years. At the end of that period, a kind of numbness had set in, like the lull before the storm, like a deafening silence, a total depletion. Imagine becoming numb and not even realizing it—not realizing it until something or someone comes along that makes you feel alive again and, better yet, passionate about being alive. I came to recognize a level of passion for life I never knew possible. Another silver lining!

Back to the surgeries-

In 2000, fighting periodic and regular seizures, Alzheimer's, and continuous falls, D was told that if he didn't consider surgery on his neck to remove three of his vertebrae, which were impinging mercilessly on nerves, that he would wake up one morning unable to walk. He braved two very serious ten-hour surgeries—one at Johns Hopkins in 2001 and one at Thomas Jefferson in 2004—each time not knowing if he would make it, but feeling certain that if he didn't, that would be better than the grim future that he would be left to confront. I say confront purposefully as D was not one to acquiesce in any situation. Living from a wheelchair with additional disabilities and having minimal if any control of body functions was not something D could relate to on any level. Given an opportunity to stop or delay more damage was a blessing. He was told that surgery would not improve his condition, but could buy him time in his decline.

As his spouse, my intent and desire was to support whatever decision D felt would bring him the most peace. I must admit I would not have had the same level of courage to proceed with the suggested surgeries. In part, it would have been due to my high level of sensitivity to medications and my personal need for more proof as to the projected outcome/success. I would have been combing the Net and any other available source, looking for the most natural route possible. I would do the same amount of research for my mate and did, but I recognized that D and I came from two different schools of thinking as to the medical field and we all know where the final decision lies.

I believe we are *all* consumers in the medical field and need to take responsible action in determining the course we choose. I have had my moments of challenging a medical recommendation and making the choice to trust my own judgment. Having this mindset, however, did not keep me from embracing D's choice and desire for what he felt was best. I have come to also appreciate the power of the mind and how important it is to believe in the choices we make. That is a good portion of the battle. It is like a facet of unconditional love, respecting where another is and giving them the support they need to *carry on* even if counter to your position.

The surgeries brought about long, painful healing periods, extreme physical compromise, exhaustive hours/days/weeks/months/years for me, endless stories of traumatic events, and probably most important, for D, a determination to rise above, until the saddest moment I can remember: May 2006, when D asked me to come sit next to him, taking my hand in his. It was a most rare moment, when he expressed his imminent desire—a desire that weighed heavy, heavy for both of us, until his final breath.

John's Hopkins Hospital and Home

John's Hopkins is where, in 2001, D had his first major ten-hour surgery to actually remove vertebrae from his cervical spine. I remember being astounded that within two days of surgery, we were in a car driving back to Norristown, Pennsylvania, from Baltimore, Maryland. That idea, for me, was most unsettling, and I didn't realize how on-target my feelings were until we arrived home.

For the uneducated eye, despite the transplant of bone (or in the instance of D's first surgery, titanium plate), an X-ray where cervical vertebrae have been removed looks like the patient's head has no inner connection to the thoracic body. It's a little unnerving and certainly makes you dubious as to one's stability and ability.

A lot of energy and time went into searching for the very right surgical team and hospital. We had our sights set on Dr. Benjamin Carson, a world-renowned head of pediatric neurosurgery at John's Hopkins … to learn that he specialized in pediatrics only. I knew it couldn't hurt to ask, being the eternal optimist that I am. What Dr. Carson did give us was a couple of good recommendations. D's surgery required both neuro- and orthopedic surgeons.

We were asked to report a day in advance and set up residence in one of the local housing areas established for families in our circumstance. What a plus arrangement that was. We semi-settled in late in the afternoon before the surgery. *Semi*, because how does one settle in under such circumstances?

By dinnertime, D became a person I did not recognize. Fear and anger were setting in, and whom do we often take our frustrations out on? At a moment when I was reaching out for closeness, not knowing what the next day would bring or if these could possibly be final hours together, there D was, running the other way. *Lord,* I prayed, *please don't let this be happening.* Did my prayer get answered? Not recognizably so.

A not recognizable answer to one's prayer perhaps *is* the answer. My faith was such, however, that I just trusted if it was meant to be different, it would be. That is not to say we always understand an answer. It does help, however, as it did in this case, to derive a smidgen of peace. I think that is a fair statement. Let's say it kept my emotions intact.

I didn't sleep at all that night, hoping that D would stir enough, mentally or physically, to reach out and just say a word or two, to touch my being or spirit somehow. It would not have mattered what the words were, or how fleeting a touch, but the silence was shattering. I was looking for added strength that I believe comes with togetherness, believing there is power in recognizing each other's hopes and pain. However, to share this experience with closeness was only an apparent heart's desire of one: *me*.

One of the few things we can be certain of is the present moment. While we are human and emotions can cause us to respond in an unfavorable manner, how we respond, for the most part, is by choice. Coming from a loving heart can always bring you peace. This is not to preclude, however, that under much duress even our strongest desires can be circumvented. This is where grace comes in, to know and understand the direction that pain can cause one to move in.

I was astounded, as D was getting ready to go into surgery, when it was announced that the hospital could not find his X-rays. We had been advised in a correspondence that they had everything they needed and we did not have to bring anything with us. I must admit, my mind was doing double-time to recall if there was any chance the X-rays were back in Philadelphia/Norristown, but I remembered the letter saying they had them. The thought that we had come this close to surgery, this far from home, and the X-rays could possibly be back in Philadelphia made me feel sick. Numb. Sick. How could this be happening?

The family had already prayed together; D was on the stretcher, ready to go into the operating room, and *this*... How could this possibly be? I couldn't allow myself to believe that the anguish we had gone through in the last twenty-four hours may have to repeat itself. Then his surgeons said they had an exact enough picture in mind of D's situation and would be willing to proceed without the X-rays; the decision was D's. My position was, *Why couldn't they take a couple emergency X-rays to provide what they needed?* Somehow, that thought was given no credence.

D's position was, "Let's just proceed." Now, why did that not surprise me? One thing was certain, it was not a decision we did or could have made together, at least as things were at that moment. Once again, I supported his decision because that was his right and was what he chose to do. I believed that the Lord was in our midst and would be throughout, just like always. That was my solace. I can't imagine what state I would have been in if I didn't have my faith to embrace.

We were all there, "the twelve disciples"—all D's siblings, children, and stepchildren, as well as my sister—praying with and for D with faith and hope, keeping a vigil during the ensuing hours.

If you have never waited for a loved one to return from surgery, a couple hours is long, but ten hours is very, very, very long. For me, there was extra anguish, for the unrest D was dealing with was still lingering as I wished him well, expressed my love, and received little to no response. The hours were long and the special waiting room was quiet with little conversation, just calls now and then from the operating room to let us know of the progress, which interrupted the deafening stillness.

As I answered the phone and listened to the words relaying the progress of surgery, all eyes turned to me. All hearing became keen. After sharing the status, each person quietly went back to their own level of solitude.

Having moved on to the thirteenth hour, we were able to see D in ICU, looking like there was little chance he would make it through the already late night. Sporadic sleep brought me into the next morning with what seemed to me an unbelievable realization. *Oh, my goodness, where are we going from here?* Back to Philadelphia, was the unsettling answer.

By now, I had learned there are times you have to move with the flow. Once certain decisions are made, there seems to be an order that takes place beyond one's control. Going back home to Norristown the second day following surgery was one of those decision in motion.

I asked my oldest son, Stephen, to accompany me in taking D back home, in total disbelief that he could even be ready to return to Norristown. I must have asked doctors the question twenty times with double question marks—those verbalized and those radiating from my baby blues: "In a traditional car?" The answer was, "Of course," with the only instruction being not to have an accident. What kind of instruction was that?

The ride seemed long and tense. What was to occur took the tension many shades higher. When we arrived home, D just wanted to lie down, so he did. Little did we know that he would not be able to get up. As he was trying to rise with whatever help I could manage, it became clear that we were not going to make it happen of our own volition. *How could this be? Nobody said this could happen.* I was anticipating a quiet, slow, and hopefully peaceful recovery.

When all else failed I sent out an SOS to D's two sons, Bruce and Rich, who lived within a half hour's ride. We carefully moved D from a lengthwise position on the bed using the bottom sheet to maneuver his body to a crosswise position. Then, with me standing in front to support his weight and keep him from falling, my stepsons raised the mattress to bring D to a standing position. It is amazing how creative you can be when a need arises and you only have your own resources to tap.

We went out the very next day and got a lift chair, which D slept in for a month before graduating to a hospital bed. Again, I queried, *How could all this be happening with no pre-warning?*

During the initial part of the recuperation period, D was unable to do anything for himself including even combing his hair. While I understood the indignities one suffers when they are in such need of another to assist them in all the daily procedures, I used to remind D that he was fortunate to have one who was willing to help to the best of her ability with a loving heart. Somehow, that did not help the frustration and anguish he was feeling.

Did we ever get back to what was our *then* normal? No. Did we get to a better place, where some peace could be grasped? I'm not sure; it would have only been momentarily. By then, the Alzheimer's symptoms were showing more and more and his gait barely improved, if at all. While we were told the surgery would not improve the gait, but would hopefully delay the guaranteed decline, it was hard to feel much hope when nothing had changed. Only the passing of time with no physical decline would convince you of the degree of success that had been reached.

We were to soon discover that D was still facing the same prognosis as when we headed down to John's Hopkins. His condition was not holding steady. A decline was becoming apparent, and thus our souls becoming more anxious.

Where to from here? This time we put our expectations in the hands of surgeons from the Rothman Institute associated with the Thomas Jefferson Hospital.

Thomas Jefferson
Hospital Stay

As D's state of stability and gait were still deteriorating, we ventured to Rothman Institute. We had gotten a very promising referral. After an exhaustive visit and evaluation, it was decided that another surgery similar to the one at Hopkins would again give D the same hope of not waking up totally paralyzed. This time, they would remove the titanium and use bone graft—bone from a bone bank and not his own bone. When one is young, they will often take bone from a hip, for the expectancy of duration is greater than if taken from a bone bank. In this instance, D was old enough that it was felt that bone from the bank should see him through his expected lifetime. Plus, it appeared the first corpectomy was not as extensive as it could have been. *Could this be? Yes, it was.*

We traveled back to John's Hopkins to evaluate their position as to further surgery, and they felt that despite the fact they saw deterioration, they did not want to operate again except as a very last resort, whatever that meant. We left Baltimore clearly aware that D would not be having a second surgery at John's Hopkins unless it was a life-or-death matter.

Another ten-hour surgery was scheduled at Thomas Jefferson, offering the same level of hope that perhaps D would once again be spared waking up one morning to find himself paralyzed.

Were we troopers now? Somehow, it didn't seem quite as frightening as the John's Hopkins experience. Did we know what to expect? We thought we did. Was it the same? *No. No. A resounding no.*

As D was wheeled into surgery with less of a contingent, this time he and I shared hopeful sentiments. As they wheeled D away and I started to the waiting room, while waiting for the elevator, I found myself leaning against a hallway window shedding involuntary and partially grateful tears; a mini, little meltdown was taking place. I knew it was in God's hands and I trusted in His ever-presence. I convinced myself what was meant to be, would be. There is something about the belief that *what is meant to be, will be* that gives one strength and hope.

It was another ten hours to wait, with intermittent calls, just like at Hopkins, to advise of progress, which was always hopeful.

The next month in the hospital was wrought with experiences. The most troubling was two days after surgery, when I finally went home to get a shower and change of clothes and a couple hours of sleep, D fell out of bed. *How could this happen?* The advocate side of me went into high gear. I was immediately on the phone with his surgeon, requesting certain stipulations in his care, including signs on his chart, signs on the walls, and "bed rails up at all times." Then I made myself ever-present for the next two weeks. D's sister, Diane, came to relieve me and was just as watchful as I was. What I found most disturbing was that regardless of the posted signs and direction of a very disgruntled surgeon, there were still times that the bed rails were left down.

I cannot express enough the importance of being very present when you have someone close to you in the hospital. Everyone needs an advocate when in the hospital. I have had doctors tell me that a family member needed to be moved on from the hospital setting to preserve well-being more than once, so you know those are not idle words. Our family has a pact to be very present when a loved one is hospitalized.

I will never forget a particular day. Diane went home after the first week, as she was a teacher and was needed in the classroom. She left on a Sunday to make the six-hour trip back to her home. Eleven hours later, when I was home getting a little rest before returning to the hospital, my doorbell rang. It was Diane, who within one hour of arriving home, turned around and came back, saying, "I couldn't leave you." She and God both knew my need.

My ever-so-caring twin, Raina, was present for me as well. Each night she, with friend Rick, would trek into the city to make certain I got home okay. They would take the train in and ride back in my car with me. Raina had heard how going home some evenings, I would almost drift into a state of limbo within a mile from my house. It was an hour-long trip each way, each day, after working all day. She never gave me the opportunity to say, "I'll be fine." She was just there, knowing what I needed. Knowing what I didn't even know I needed.

The expression, "Little things mean a lot" warranted a song. It's so true—especially for caregivers. Little things do mean a lot. While in the hospital for the month, D contracted a fungal infection in the blood stream and a strep infection, at which time it was determined he needed to be out of the hospital once his fever came down. One day I was walking back to D's hospital room, discouraged that the fever he had was hanging on and that little progress was being exhibited. I just wanted to vent. Vent? What does that mean? How does one do that? For me, it was a shoulder to cry on (not literally). Anyway, at that very moment I received a phone call from a caring friend. Speak of timing. I was learning more and more the meaning of timing. I needed that phone call like one needs whatever they need when they need it. All right, not the best analogy, I know … but that was the feeling.

As if what was happening was not enough, during this time, due to pains in his legs, it was discovered that D had major blood clots in both of his legs. Due to the hematomas, they could not put D on a blood thinner and he wouldn't survive surgery, so a mesh stint was put in the vena cava (the main artery leading from both legs), to not allow the blood clots to pass beyond a certain point. To complete this picture, D was also put on a feeding tube, due to some difficulties he was having in swallowing.

In what appeared to be a somewhat unstable state, and because the doctors were concerned about his safety to remain in the hospital, D was being moved to Bryn Mawr Rehab, miles from center city. It seemed extremely important to him that someone follow his ambulance to his new location. Normally, I would have been the natural candidate; however, I had suffered a panic attack years before and avoided the Schuylkill Expressway with a *passion*.

I always got to where I needed to be, but in my way. And, of course, we all know the ambulance was not going to be going my way. No words held that much magic. I called everyone I could think of to participate in this venture, but to no avail. *Alas*, into the car I got, shaking with doubt as I followed the ambulance. There was no way I was going to let another vehicle come between me and that ambulance or let that ambulance get out of my sight. *Lord*, I prayed, *please wrap your arms around me this time and slow my racing heart.*

I tried to focus on D in the ambulance to keep my body from shaking and keep my thoughts on how important it was to him that I was doing this. I thought that once I was on the Schuylkill, I would find some comfort: so much for that! The anxiety just became more profound. Now my mind and heart were both racing. How could I have agreed to this? Is there anyone else in this world I would be doing this for? D seemed so vulnerable. I had queried of him, "Do you really feel like you need someone following the ambulance?" There was no hesitation in his affirmative answer. Well, perhaps I could see this as a growth experience, or perhaps it would be an experience that would keep me forever from the Schuylkill.

As we arrived closer to Bryn Mawr, at least an hour-plus trip from center city, the ambulance was going faster and faster. I had clearly begged them not to lose sight of me and to maintain a reasonable speed. There was no question in my mind that halfway into the trip, I had become one of any other car on the road. In my panic, prayer, no conscious prayer, peeked in only sporadically. Perhaps it takes having felt major panic to understand that statement. It was like all my senses were being called on to maneuver through the experience.

At Bryn Mawr, my heart settled a little, though I must admit I wasn't sure what would bring it back to a normal beat. Having MVP sometimes, it could take weeks to not experience the missed beats stirred by anxious moments. There was no way this experience did not push the limits.

Well, the Bryn Mawr Rehab stay was a month long and, such as it was, still an hour each way, each day, to see D and check on his care. He made a little progress in rehab, but not enough for them to keep him or send him home. *Now what?* It was suggested that he go into a nursing home and the decision of where, was the Saunder's House by Lankenau Hospital—another month of continued care and more therapy. The Saunder's House's logistics still spelled an hour each way, each day, after work.

We did have one celebration of progress at Bryn Mawr before leaving. D was able to have the feeding tube removed. Did we party! *Party* because D could now go back to eating. If you've ever had the experience of watching D eat, you know what a party that was.

Once at the Saunder's House, some admittance testing was done, and they said that D tested positive to TB. They started to treat him for that, though there were no symptoms and there is always question of a false positive test; eventually he was taken off of that medication.

D never found any peace at the Saunder's House, for I believe by this time he was feeling like he would never get home, which I totally understood. I, too, was beginning to feel like he would never return home.

On one occasion/outing, I brought him home, knowing he had to return later in the day. Upon needing to leave to go back to the nursing home, I realized what a *mistake* I had made. Well, almost mistake. Understandably, D did not want to return to the nursing home, and if you don't know what an immovable object looks like, you needed to be with us that day. While I knew I would not plan another like venture, I was still happy he was able to be at home for a short while. It was reassuring to know that he would soon be returning home somewhat improved and those trips back and forth would come to a halt. Those were the words I used to coax him into returning for just a few more weeks.

During this three-month period, I was working in a fast-paced law firm that required my utmost attention during the day, and visiting D each evening caused me to experience a depletion of energy I was not familiar with. But remember, I am a survivor.

I have since come to see myself as a "winner." The experience does not have to change, just the way we perceive it. What changes is the sense of staying on top as opposed to working your way to the top.

While at Saunder's House, each Sunday we would visit a local church and go out to lunch, as D was getting stronger. Finally, we were told he could return home. Talk about mixed emotions! The best part, the very best part, was that traveling one hour each way, each day, for three months was over. *Yes, over… really over.* And now D could be at home, in his familiar surroundings, and we would discover what level of normalcy existed for him and for me.

I came home each day at lunch to make sure he was eating. I would always leave breakfast on a tray with the daily newspaper and then prepare him lunch at noon. On one of those trips home, he was mentioning (he never complained) a pain on the right side of his upper chest area. It was not quite in the heart area, but I felt it needed to be checked. Much against his will, I called his family doctor, who advised me to take D to the emergency room and said that he would meet us there. D was admitted for observation, at which time it was felt he needed to be sent to Lankenau Hospital for a heart catheterization. They found one artery 90 percent blocked and another artery 80 percent blocked with a blood clot. He was admitted to Lankenau and spent five days, on a special medication (Plavix), waiting for the clot to dissolve so they could put stints in his heart—a procedure known as "angioplasty."

Could we dare anticipate improvement in our lives at this point? I say "anticipate" because it is a choice whether we see the glass as half-full or half-empty. I prefer the former, but I must admit to moments of transposing that image. Would this be one of those moments? If it was, it would be short-lived.

Last Trip— A Wedding Beaconed

I Dos—I Did, Alas

It was January, 2006.

The event: Wedding bells for Stephen, my oldest son, and Kim.

The place: Des Moines, Iowa.

By this time, traveling had become slightly challenging, as D could no longer walk the kind of distances required in an airport; also being stationary in a car for a period of time exacerbated his condition.

However, more important than all of that, D very much wanted to attend the wedding of Stephen and Kim. He and Stephen had become close over the years, and this was an event that he did not want to miss.

The only question was what was the best way to make the trip, taking into consideration that D's strength and mobility were definitely compromised, as well as some of his reasoning powers. I learned rather quickly along our journey that few situations are all that simplistic and many facets are often at play.

There was a part of me that wanted to go away and enjoy Stephen and Kim's wedding without a care in the world. Sound a little selfish? It wasn't meant to, but perhaps it was the result of catering to a situation for almost six years, even though it was done with heartfelt concern, affection, and attention. Every now and then, there is something that we want to give our total, undivided attention to. Nevertheless, another side prevailed and that was recognizing that I wanted D to have the same opportunity to be a part of this event, which was special for him as well, and I wanted us to share in this happy occasion. To have it any other way would have gone against my own philosophy that all my decisions be made to where I would feel no qualms.

It was decided that a car trip would be too long and not comfortable enough; that left air flight. I knew conditions were such that I would want some support to help with D. He would need a wheel chair to get through the airport and other help, as well. My youngest son, Richard, made the flight with us.

It's at times like this that you realize how much others can be present for you. I clearly knew my son was making a concession to fly without his directly saying so, but he recognized the need, which he gave more credence to than his preference. For me, this was huge.

I was amazed at how going through security differed for D as compared to Richard and me. Richard and I kind of sailed right on through, but D, despite being in a wheel chair, was scrutinized. As I watched them take off his shoes, his jacket, his belt, and his hat, I couldn't help but wonder if they didn't realize how redoing what they were undoing would be twice the task? We knew such scrutiny was not necessary; why couldn't security see that? Yes, I know that is not a logical question on my part, but we were not talking about a speedy process here and we had little time to spare to make our flight. However, I do know that at times, it is best just to be still. Plus, I knew that D would not appreciate any interjection from me. One of those "silence is golden moments" was at play.

We spent a long weekend in Des Moines going though a number of wedding events.

It was a happy time, laced with some concerns. This is where the reasoning aspect I mentioned earlier came into play.

Along with the mother of the bride and bridesmaids, I had gone out to have a manicure on the afternoon before the rehearsal dinner, which was the night before the wedding. I had asked D, with strong suggestion, to wait to get a shower and change for the dinner until I returned, which would be in plenty of time. "Please wait," I asked. "Please?"

His response was silence. Now, this silence lead to mental questioning on my part, but I knew I needed to keep moving forward with the plans of the day and that was the best response I could hope for. In these instances, silence did not denote a specific yes or no. It literally left you not knowing, no further along than before the conversation took place. But I would just say, *Please God, let my words register.*

I was sensitive to the frustration D must have experienced in feeling like he should have to respond to such a request. This is when reasoning fell short, with Alzheimer's weighing on the situation. Though I must admit, it was very difficult at times to determine what was beyond his control and what wasn't. Was disability at play or resentment? I always preferred to err on the side of "beyond one's control."

When I returned to our suite, I called to D as I went through the main door, receiving no response. I called out another quick hi, to no avail. I had come to realize that a lack of response did not have to bring reason for concern. But then again, how could I be certain? So I hurried to the bedroom area and found D in the bathroom attempting to shave. As I looked at him, I was shocked and concerned to see that the whites of both of his eyes were very red. Not pink, *red.* D had fairly dark brown eyes, and the whites were almost as deep a red as the brown was brown.

"What happened, hon?" I asked.

He responded, "Why?"

"Look at your eyes, D," I replied, not having any idea as to what might be infringing on his body at that moment. Wasn't there already enough?

After another query, he responded that he had decided not to wait to take a shower. While in the shower, he fell and had been able to hold on to a vertical handicap bar with untold strength, the kind you find when there is no hope of its existence. Well, he was holding on so tightly, "afraid to let go," for what appeared to be an unbelievable amount of time, that it caused the blood vessels in his eyes to rupture. In a hundred years, I would have never guessed that to be the cause of what I was observing. He did somehow get himself from the bathroom to the bedroom to rest until he had enough energy to shave. I knew it had been a harrowing experience for him, for otherwise, he would have never been explicit in reiterating the event.

We proceeded to the rehearsal dinner, got through the evening, and moved on to the wedding day. We were halfway through the weekend, with the most important part yet to be.

My biggest concern at the wedding was that we were going to be walking up three steps and lighting a candle together and then back down the steps. For a healthy person, it would be a cakewalk. But I had concern looming in the back of my mind. What if D tripped on the stairs? What if a candle got accidentally knocked over? My having been badly burned when I was fourteen just magnified that concern. But guess what ... We went through the process just like it was a *piece of cake*.

We went through the next day and the trip back home rather smoothly as well; I was grateful.

D and I took few vacations: London, Bermuda, Nassau (two times), Santa Fe, New Mexico, and Hilton Head,

South Carolina. That was it over a twenty-year period, and those were all before the last eight years of our marriage. There is an old adage that goes: "*Don't put off* until *tomorrow* what *you* could *do today*." We often talked about taking more vacations, but we put off that which would never happen, for there was no tomorrow. Enjoy those things that call to you, *when they call to you*.

I want to share a story I recently heard that touches on this concept.

A gentleman was riding along in his hometown, from one meeting to another. As he was traveling the familiar road, he saw a sign that was posted by a travel agency. It portrayed a scenic Scandinavian country with a lovely-looking young woman enjoying the beautiful countryside. He passed the sign, but the vision lingered, and he found himself going back. Before he knew it, that same day, he had responded to their offer for a Scandinavian vacation, which turned out to be a wonderful venture. At the time he signed up, he had not been contemplating a vacation at all. Now, whether it was the beautiful countryside or the lovely-looking young woman that caught his fancy was immaterial. What mattered was that he responded to a desire, be it sudden or otherwise, which in turn caused him to learn about another part of our world and the differences that abound from one area to another, from one culture to another. A cherished memory was created. The life he is now living is a little richer because he ventured forth, because he did not say "Maybe tomorrow."

We have no way of knowing when an opportunity will be whisked away, never to return. However, we do know when an opportunity presents itself that the moment is ours to seize or not. This is not meant to be pessimistic but rather optimistic. Why not experience as many cherished moments as you can possibly make in your life?

Bon Voyage!

Last Day at Home

*You Know When You
Know That You Know*

The last day at home did not happen in a day.

I lost my job in the midst of all the preceding events, knowing we needed my income at this time and having been unable to find another job immediately. I was then sixty-five, not an age when one looks very desirable to most employers. I found a temporary job at the company where my daughter-in-law worked. I was excited and concerned at the same time. It seemed like D needed someone with him more and more, though he would not affirm that. I was also aware of how much we needed the extra financial boost.

Need dictated. *Which need?* It felt like a push-pull situation. I made my decision, knowing that by not working, it would add a negative tone to other needs. Plus, D at this time was rather stationary in his daily activities, and I would ask someone to come in each day and check on him. I could just imagine how much he was going to love that, but we each need to find our peace.

It is crucial when you are centered on helping one through an all-consuming, time-absorbing situation that you do not lose your own identity and that you hold out for the things that speak to your values, your emotional sanity, and a portion of peace. So I accepted the position, reasoning that it would not be for long, only a temporary situation that would allow me to totally consider what it would mean for "us" if I found a full-time position. It gave me a chance to wrap my mind around how working full time would impact us. •

Each morning I would make D breakfast and lunch, making certain his hot coffee and newspapers were front and center, then I would leave for work. It was too far for me to come home at lunchtime.

At this juncture, there was still an occasional day when I arrived home at the end of the workday and he would be sitting there in jacket and hat, wanting me to take him into the office. Conversation had waned, but we were still in sync. This would be one of those moments, for I knew what he was wanting. What tenacity he had. He could not function beyond reading the newspaper, perhaps looking at a filing, but he felt the need to keep his ship afloat. I begged him on a few occasions to let go and let others help him. Let go and trust that God would bring about what needed to happen to make the transition smooth. I guess when you have lived something so intensely as he did his career, letting go is more difficult than might be imagined. Perhaps letting go only comes when it is no longer your choice. Thus it became no longer a choice. Actually, on these couple of occasions, D would go no farther than the door and turn around to return to his recliner.

Talk about mixed emotions. I would be relieved that he was not able, and sad that he was going through this experience. I suspect this was a kind of torment for him.

Here we were that day in May, when D asked me to sit next to him on the bed. He took my hand in his and shared feelings that resounded in my being over and over and over again. He wanted me to know that he hoped God would be merciful to him and that his life was becoming too difficult for him to want to continue. My heart ached. I heard his words, I felt his words, I assimilated his words, but I had no words—no words that made any sense at that moment. I put my arm around him and just held him close, wanting him to know I was by his side no matter what. I was reassured that he received my message, for he melted into my embrace.

I am not usually rendered speechless, but at this instant, I was. I heard, I felt, and I understood what he was saying. I say I "understood," but as I have gazed back over those moments so many times, I'm not certain I totally understood. I certainly heard him; I certainly felt for him; but did I truly understand?

As time and medical procedures ensued, I often wondered how well I did understand. *What I did learn* was that I could not be responsible for making any decision that would feel like I was taking D's life. I *also learned* that I needed God more than ever. We became a hand-in-hand and heart-to-heart experience from henceforth.

From that moment on, everything at home changed. D no longer seemed to want to get up or eat. When I would suggest taking him to see his family doctor, the response was simple for him: "Sloan, there is no discussion." When I would suggest any doctor of his choosing, the response was still simple: "Sloan, I told you how I feel." On a couple occasions, as he would be lying in bed, not responsive to much around him, my request was answered simply, "Sloan," with an admonishing tone. It was clear he was saying, *I am not going anywhere for help. I don't want that kind of help.*

Was he asking me to just sit by and watch him slowly die—die because I did not get him help? The end result was that I knew I had to live with myself as well.

Let me tell you, this proved to be the most difficult, emotionally challenging, heart-wrenching area of this six-year journey. My questions to myself: Was D saying, "I want God to bring my life to an end as quickly as is within his will"? *Or* was D saying, "I need you not to do anything that will in any way prolong my existence, regardless"? I guess it was a little of each.

Why do I say "regardless"? For me, there were issues that spoke to what would be my call and what would be God's call. Yes, they were often fine lines, but nonetheless the question remained. I knew I needed a stronger-than-strong conviction with the sense of God's nudging to convince me.

So I had decided to call the family doctor and see what options there were. At this point, a week had not gone by since our heartfelt exchange. I was driving home from my temporary job and I tried calling D, just to check in to see how he was doing, something I frequently did. There was no answer. *No answer?* I tried again. *No answer.* An uneasiness flooded my being that caused me to hurry as fast as I possibly could to arrive home. When I did, I hurriedly entered the house and went straight to the bedroom. Why did our hallway seem longer than ever before?

D was in bed, nothing touched on his breakfast/lunch tray, and I realized he had not gotten up all day. I tried to get him to sit up and drink something and realized he was very, very weak and unable to walk. He had needed to get up, but I am not certain he even tried. Dehydration had set in.

I called for help to get him to the hospital. He didn't want to go. He asked not to go, *but* he had to go. I would have been the one ending his life if he didn't go. It was clear to me that while it was a possible option theoretically, it was not a choice that I had. My soul was crying, *Please, Lord, may your will be done.*

As the ambulance attendants were taking D out of the house, the rain was streaming down. His son, Richard, and brother, Tom, were there. I had called for their help because the day had taken a toll far greater than I alone could handle, at which time it became crystal clear that an ambulance was needed. As I closed the door of the house behind us that evening, I remember feeling like the raindrops were teardrops all around me, for my heart was crying out. I related to the moment we were experiencing and not that D might never come through that door again, *in* or *out*—but I wonder if somehow I knew.

One question that later came to mind: If I had called a doctor to see him at home, might he have been able to be treated in a hospice-like situation, allowing his life to slowly dwindle away without all the agony we faced in the next eight months? Of course, this is sheer speculation and more than likely would not have been the way it would have unfolded in any regard. I had chosen not to second-guess myself, for I continually functioned from a place of love, concern, and prayerful expectation.

All and all, I do have the belief that God is in charge, and when it was D's time, he would be taken home to be with our Lord. I also realize that we are given choices and God helps us through the choices we make. Oh, how I prayed. But certain choices seemed like I was taking it out of God's hands.

I was grateful that D was not like the shoemaker who didn't repair his family's shoes, but did repair everyone else's. He did have a Living Health Directive that was referred to a number of times throughout the ensuing eight months. Even having this document made decisions difficult, but it allowed for a level of assurance one could not have otherwise. But the system is not perfect, and things happened that probably shouldn't have. Why do I say *probably* shouldn't have? Because of my belief that all things happen with reason.

D arrived at Montgomery Hospital Emergency only to be transported to Temple Hospital brain trauma, as a CAT scan revealed several hematomas. His path from that point never brought him back home. Our home became a place where I would go to retire at the end of a wearisome day, a place to find solace, a place to regain strength, a place to occasionally let the all-too-seldom tears flow, a place to speak out loud to God, and a place to rest into the morning with hope in my heart. My hope was for continued strength and peace for D and continued strength and peace for me.

So we moved with the moment, we started another leg of our journey, and we prayed for continued strength and peace along our path.

The Final Hospital Call

Is the End Around the Corner?

I do not know when in my life I have experienced more anguish, being literally panic-stricken, barely recognizing myself, having to make two decisions that undoubtedly changed the course of "our" life, over the next eight months. My mind was doing somersaults, with my body feeling prickly all over and a sense that I couldn't feel the floor under my feet, yet everything I needed to be doing was happening.

It was a lunch hour, and I was on my way to see D at Gwynedd Square Nursing Home.

That last day he had spent at home ended with him being sent from the emergency room at Montgomery Hospital to Temple Hospital—Temple Hospital, because of their brain trauma center. The surgeons at Temple said they wanted the hematomas to liquefy before draining, which would be the most minimal procedure for his condition. They wanted D in a nursing home while he waited for a few weeks before going back to Temple to have the hematomas drained. If they tried to remove them in a gelled state, it would mean surgery—a craniotomy—that they felt he would definitely not survive.

I remember so clearly my conversation with the representative from Temple when she told me that D needed to go into a nursing home. He and I had been in many during our period of serving on the deacon board with our church, and I knew not all nursing homes are alike. I proceeded to tell the social worker that it couldn't be just any nursing home, that I needed to be able to go home at night and put my head on my pillow and rest, knowing that he was in the best place available to us. She sent me to Gwynedd Square Nursing Home, and I felt very comfortable with what I saw, and so the decision was made.

During this initial period at Gwynedd, there was definite regression in D's speech and response patterns, swallowing being one of the main areas. The speech therapist is the one who addresses this area. Her summation was that D was very cognitively impaired and was processing very slowly, but he would repeat frequently (not clearly or always audibly) to help process, and as to swallowing, she had major concerns and felt there were a lot of red flags. At the time they were doing what was referred to as "blower therapy" (using air to trigger the swallowing reflex) to protect his airway and to improve his voice volume, all of which never really happened. The speech therapist recommended pureed food because of questionable swallowing issues. I made every effort to be there at meal times, as I was, for the most part, the only one he would respond to in consuming those indefinable mounds of color.

Decision One

On one of my lunch hours while driving the familiar route to see D, I received a phone call that he was being transported from Gwynedd to Montgomery's Emergency because he had aspirated while eating. I changed my course and hurried to Montgomery Hospital. I arrived in advance of the ambulance and decided to wait at the point where they would be bringing him into the emergency room, praying that it was indeed the right place.

After what seemed like an endless wait, the stretcher was wheeled in. D was motionless but with eyes open. I tried to get his attention, but there was no response. My senses told me that what was happening was definitely something different than aspiration. Now, I knew little about the results of one aspirating, but something wasn't making sense and I had learned to trust my senses. They did an emergency CAT and discovered the condition of the hematomas were such that he needed emergency surgery. I was told that if he was not intubated, he would not make it to Temple, which is where the surgical team would be waiting his arrival.

The clock was ticking, ticking, ticking. Why couldn't it stop for a minute? Just one minute, please.

The word "intubation" brought about immediate panic. D had already said how he felt, and yet the emergency room doctor was trying to assure me that depending on how things … no, *regardless* of how things went at Temple, the breathing tube could always be removed; it was a temporary measure just to get him to Temple. I was not convinced. Even if I had been, should that be my decision alone?

I knew I had to reach D's three children and see how they felt, and I only had an instant to do that. I was grateful for no delays in making those contacts. I had already talked to my son, Stephen, who just happened to be calling before I called him, and he arrived at the hospital in minutes. D's brother, Tom, who lives in the area, came to the hospital as well.

How do I make this instant decision to intubate D? How do I make this instant decision not to intubate D? It felt like there was no time for thinking or for evaluating facts, *no time* to make a decision. That sounds strange, doesn't it? For me, a "decision" denotes that for which you have time to determine the facts and possibilities, otherwise what do you have? Perhaps a happening.

D's youngest son arrived at the hospital, his daughter and oldest son lived further away and planned to go right to Temple. Richard, Tracey, and Bruce all felt they wanted the intubation procedure and caringly asked me what I wanted, as well, while I kept hearing D's words that he did not want to continue his life as it was. We all knew what he had expressed, but was this the moment to end all procedures? Was this an act of heroism? It was like action was going on all around me and somehow I was a part of it, but I could barely formulate an answer.

I had always taken a position with my stepchildren that the love they had for their father, while different from mine, was just as important, and I intended to honor and respect these relationships. It mattered very much to me what they felt and desired in terms of decisions about their father's care. There is no way it could not be a part of the equation.

There was a caveat, however. Because of the condition of D's cervical spine (no vertebrae and grafting), he had no flexibility, which made placing a breathing tube extremely difficult, possibly impossible. I repeat, *possibly impossible*. Might that be a saving grace for D? Oh, how I prayed that if it wasn't meant to be, the team would not be able to complete the procedure. Just at that point, they were about to give up. I could hear their conversation as I paced outside the room he was in. I had also become aware that the responses to pain I heard from D had ceased. *The answer*—he was intubated and ready to go.

We followed the critical care ambulance to Temple, not being permitted to ride in it. I rode with my son. Actually, we didn't follow them for long or we, too, would have been breaking the rules of the road. When we arrived at Temple, we were asked to wait. We were not allowed to see D, but we were told we would be meeting with the surgeons momentarily.

I will never forget during that momentary wait, one of the deacons-in-training at our church arrived to support our family. I can't remember how he knew we were there, but what I did know was that God was always bringing us what we needed when we needed it. At that moment, he shared with me that the Deacon Board would be giving me a check to help with expenses. While that was the furthest thing from my thought processes at that moment, he knew it would help to alleviate a concern, which it did; my heart was grateful. They knew D had not been able to work and that I had been out of work for a time as well. Again, God's timing was impeccable. I had received another silver lining in the midst of a storm.

With gratitude I wrote

Dear Deacons,

I have wanted to write this note long before now, but hadn't been able to find words adequate enough to tell you how very grateful I am, how blessed I feel, and how your gracious generosity will remain in my treasury of memories as long as I live.

God's loving arms reached out to me through your ministry and gave me yet another testimony. No matter how grim things may appear when you are not certain God can possibly focus on your many challenges and pain, He appears in your life (where He has been all along), envelopes you with his presence, and meets a need; and I know the difference between desire and need.

Your ministry is a perfect example of God's work in progress. Siloam is very blessed to have such a deacon's board, and I am very blessed to have such a caring church family. I have been at Siloam for almost nineteen years now; my first Sunday was, September 27, 1987, as Mrs. Richard Rogers. I was warmly greeted then and that warmth has only grown. I love you all, and I know Dick would join me in that sentiment.

The gift you gave is being used judiciously in meeting needs that Dick and I encounter along the way. Thank you so very much. With love and prayer that each of you and your families be wonderfully blessed, indeed.

Sis Sloan

Decision Two

Now we were being led into a conference room right outside of emergency. The surgeons told us that they would try to drain the hematomas, but if they were not successful, that would mean a craniotomy that D would not survive. They were marginally positive about the draining procedure. We were taken in to see D, and I cannot put into words how sad and distressed I felt. One only had to look at him to know he was hanging between life and death.

We were given a moment to review his Living Health Directive with the hospital's social worker, and a decision was made. I told the surgeons if the draining worked, we would proceed from that point, but if more extensive surgery was required, they were not to go forward. The Living Health Directive was a saving grace of sorts, for based on all our interpretations, what had happened thus far would have been in accord with what D had designated legally. At least, that is what we convinced ourselves to believe.

What I had become painfully aware of is that what one denotes in a Living Health Directive can change based on circumstances that may not have been perceived in the designating process, but in any regard, it is the best we have available to us.

Once again, we were waiting, praying, and anticipating. A couple of hours had passed when D was wheeled into ICU. In the early morning hours my stepson took me home, though reluctantly, but I had to get my own car, which was still parked at Montgomery Hospital's Emergency lot, and I really did need to sleep, if possible, as we were now going on twenty-four hours of no rest.

Within a day and a half, D was sitting up, eating, and communicating. There was even a lilt in his voice. This seemed monumental. That night I went home with a lighter spirit than I had had in weeks. I was actually relieved that he seemed so well and that perhaps all of our decisions were being rewarded, and D could still experience some meaningful existence. Hope was welling.

Then, within another day, something happened—a major regression. D stopped eating, was less responsive, and had multiple seizures, one right after another (six within less than an hour). Again, the surgeon reviewed the CAT scans with me, met with the family, and determined there was nothing more that D would be able to withstand and that he could go at any time. We cried, we prayed for no suffering, and we waited; D hung on.

I met with the nursing staff to make certain, as the surgeon did, that his chart was clearly highlighted and marked that no special/additional support measures were to be taken. *Not anything!*

Later, when I was walking back in his room, I couldn't believe when I heard that he had been given a transfusion. *What was happening here?* Plus, a nasal feeding tube had been placed. *Was this for real? How could this be? Didn't it matter what was marked on his chart? And they didn't even ask. Now what?*

That wasn't all. As I walked into ICU a couple days later, I was asked to put on a gown and gloves as D had contracted MRSA staph in the bloodstream. Then came a message that it was important to get him out of the hospital. I had heard that message before.

As wonderfully important as the medical arena is, we must realize that it is not infallible. Many mistakes, often traumatic ones, happen in hospitals on a daily basis, and infections are quite prevalent in that environment. So while we can derive hope in procedures that must take place in a hospital, we need to stay very much a part of the process or have an advocate there to support us.

Well, I was very happy that Gwynedd would take D back with the MRSA staph, but they kept him isolated. I knew he had been in the hospital for the last time.

It has been a while since I mentioned D's perseverance and strong will; he did overcome the MRSA staph.

Anger isn't something I feel very often, based on my non-judgmental view of things, but I found myself rather frustrated when having to make the decision to change

D's nasal feeding tube to that of an abdominal/stationary one before he could be moved back to Gwynedd. This was something that if instructions had been followed, I would not have to be discussing. I could make the determination not to put a feeding tube in place, but to withdraw one that was already placed had a whole different impact.

The doctor he had at Gwynedd was so caring. As soon as D arrived back to the nursing home, his doctor sat down with me for almost an hour to review D's chart, the Living Health Directive, and my expectations. He was troubled that the feeding tube had been placed without consent and felt that it was more than he would have wanted. He did tell me he would remove it, but I just couldn't make that call. It was decided that we would revisit the choice in three months. *Three months* at that moment sounded like eternity. I prayed—prayed fervently for God's will to be done.

I have tried to make sense of the next months that followed. I am a believer that all things happen with reason. It is amazing the meaning we can find in happenings, the solace that we can construct as we move through what seems like a senseless period.

A Caretender's Meltdown

What Is One's Limit?

What causes one to melt down? I have always found that an interesting expression—"melt down." Now I see it as a saturation point needing an outlet that can't be denied and is not limited to age.

It was a beautiful fall day with a slight chill in the air as I pulled out of my driveway with package in hand and a slightly light heart. I no longer recall the content intended for delivery. However, I do not forget my destination. I was stopping by some dear friends from my church to deliver that name-less package. This couple was only ever a phone call away and periodically checked with me to let me know they were present, loving me, and ready to help. They had taken me under their wings. Yes, like angels.

This was a rare moment, for I usually didn't take time to do much else other than to go to work and visit with D until it was almost time to end my day. This was an exceptional day, in which I was allowing myself some special time to say hi to some folks who meant so much to me.

As I ventured to their home, I felt a slight lightness of spirit. It was an instant of feeling like this moment was mine.

When I think of saturation, I think of any item unable to hold any more fluid. I discovered what it meant to be emotionally saturated on this beautiful fall day.

I got out of my car and proceeded to hurry to the door. As I did, I tripped and experienced a fall, somewhat braced by my arms reaching out in front of me. Unable to get up (I did try several times), I called for help as the neighbors were busily mowing their lawns, drowning out my cries. And *cry* I did. Realizing that my calls for help seemed futile, I was hoping the leaf-blowing neighbor would just see me; he didn't need to hear me. How, *how*, could he not see me? Would I have seen him, if it was in reverse?

There was a momentary flash of how D would have experienced this particular fall, being unable to brace himself, for even with my doing that, I could feel the sting of scrapes on my face and the loosening of my very front teeth. Even though my right arm felt too traumatized to lift my weight, I still knew I was better off than if I had not had the use of my arms. Yes, the tears continued to flow, and flow, and flow some more.

My friends, realizing I had not yet arrived, looked out to see me on the ground. Upon helping me up, it was decided that I needed to go to the hospital. I cried all the way, with one apology after another, tears and apologies flowing simultaneously, endlessly.

And cry I did. For an unbelievable four hours straight, I was apologizing my way through triage, the emergency room, and the X-ray room. Tears flowed uncontrollably, not gut-wrenchingly, but definitely apparent. If my sister had not joined me at the hospital and explained that my life's circumstances were venting, I'm not certain what they would have thought. I guess it would not have mattered at that moment, anyhow.

Did I feel better after the deluge of tears? I don't remember; I just know it was necessary at that given moment and probably helped me get through the next period of time.

By this point, not only was *nothing* easy, but D's fight for survival took precedence over all, *all the time*. Our relationship was about D surviving his ill fate and my surviving the experience of being there to help him through each inch ... literally each inch of the way. But it probably wasn't survival that D was fighting for, but dying with dignity.

As if this wasn't enough ...

My meltdown harbored a number of happenings.

In 2004, it was suggested I should have half my thyroid removed, as they wanted to rule out the possibility of cancer. After going through what was very painful testing and receiving what was considered not conclusive results, I proceeded to seek the advice of a couple surgeons. At one of the surgeon's suggestions, I went for a follow-up echogram. In retesting the cysts on the one-half of my thyroid, some were now discovered on the other side. After a moment of fear and serious concern in evaluating all the information, I knew I needed to keep my faith and continue to trust that God was in charge and would somehow bring me to the right decision. I felt I could not deal with one more anguished moment than I was already experiencing and that which I knew to be forthcoming. Even my doctors and surgeons felt I needed to postpone any surgery at that given time, as D was due for his second major surgery.

In passing, now five years later, I discovered that cysts on the thyroid are quite common with Hashimoto's. I am still trusting this is what I have. We sent the tissue from my biopsies to Thomas Jefferson, John's Hopkins, and Sloan Kettering. There were no conclusive results or emphatic recommendations. I am at peace.

As if this wasn't enough…

The last year and a half of D's illness, I lost my job and was quite concerned. That was in September of 2005. How would we make it financially with all the medical expenses? Even though we had insurance, his medicine alone was several hundred a week. This was when I *learned* the meaning of, "in God's time."

I was so earnest about finding work that I would get up every morning, dress for a job (the one I didn't yet have), check the newspapers and Web sites, make calls to set up appointments with employment agencies, go for interviews, and visit potential employers on a daily basis. I even had a couple personal referrals thrown in the mix. Ones who knew me and had sent me on an interview would comment, "We don't understand, Sloan, why you haven't been hired." I didn't either, at the time—the operative words here being, "*at the time.*"

However, during this period, D suffered a number of serious issues with hematomas from his many falls, and he really needed extra care with the aftermath of a couple surgeries and going from home to hospital to nursing home. *Then* one bright, sunshiny day, I had an interview for a position that came from my resume being given to an administrative director by a dear friend from church, at the company where he worked. I was hired instantly and started work less than a week after my interview. The same day I started work, D was transferred from the hospital to a nursing home only five minutes from where I would be working. Could it get any better, under the circumstances? I thought not and I still think not. In 2004, I had spent a period of three months traveling an hour each way, each day after work to visit D.

My new employment was meant to be; it was in the making all along. This was the most striking event in my life bringing me to appreciate the saying, "In God's time."

Thank you, Lord. Things were looking up and that was my only meltdown.

Special Events at Gwynedd

What Makes a Difference?

I always felt I had made a very good choice as to Gwynedd Square Nursing Home, where D received his final care.

I sent the following note to them upon D's demise:

> To All Those At Gwynedd Square: the entire office staff, social services, nurses, aides, therapists, and everyone else who touched the life of Richard Rogers,

Some time has passed since the passing of my husband, Dick Rogers, but not the gratefulness I feel for all the special care he received at Gwynedd Square.

When I received the call from Temple University Hospital that Dick needed to go into a nursing home, I remember my first words, "It can't be just any nursing home," and it wasn't. Gwynedd was a blessing in the midst of pain. Your home far surpassed my greatest expectation in every way. Dick was treated with great care and attention in meeting his medical, mental, and physical needs; you honored the whole person. *And* the same caring hearts that tended to Dick's needs so patiently supported me and other family members as well.

Almost every day, Dick was gotten up and dressed, and was provided as much stimulation as possible; he was given therapy as long as absolutely feasible. The nursing staff was so very attentive to his every need. Time was taken to answer many questions and many phone calls at all different hours. Special attention with utmost respect was given to family concerns at patient planning meetings. Dick was welcomed back from Temple Hospital after a longer stay than usual in isolation. When Dick was given a roommate, it was with forethought. The support of hospice was welcomed and encouraged and the list goes on.

I was also very touched by different events/experiences: How you encouraged and supported our giving Dick what turned out to be his last birthday party; the entertainment/games/crafts provided for the residents; the Sunday devotional services;

the friendly greetings constantly flowing; *and* the never-to-be-forgotten New Year's Eve party, 2006.

How would I spend a meaningful New Year's Eve with my husband? *That was my question.* You all made it wonderful. The spirit was so radiant that I truly almost forgot where I was. I went home that New Year's evening with a sense of joy.

I remember thinking that Dick may be with us another year. Little did I know that in sixteen short days, I would be starting the most painful journey of my life. However, I do have peace that Dick is at rest and that he had the very best possible care until the Lord took him home.

I will be forever thankful.

Sloan

What Made A Difference?

A Birthday Party

This brings to mind a feeling that has lingered with me in the realm of slight regrets, which I tried ardently to keep at bay. Five months before D passed away, we had a birthday party for him at the nursing home. He was in a wheel chair, unable to communicate for the most part, but certainly aware of his surroundings. He had been put on a feeding tube after surgery at Temple, due to his inability to respond to eating. During the party, he asked for some lemonade and cake as best he could; the request was discernable. In my mode to protect D from possible aspiration, he was not given any lemonade or cake—a decision that was made at a patient care meeting. The thought of pleasure eating had been considered and vetoed.

A side note: When one is on a feeding tube, they can have pureed types foods on special occasions, which is called "pleasure eating." At the patient's planning meeting, it was expressed that D was at greater risk of aspiration than is often the case and therefore, we would forego that risk. I explained the decision to D at the time it was made.

D and I had had a quasi-conversation when he had been on pureed foods, and he appeared to agree that he did not want to take a risk of aspirating. At this period, he had little conversation, mostly responses, so the right questions had to be asked not to influence his thinking and then there was the question of "judgment," due to the Alzheimer's. Even though D had major difficulty in communicating, I totally respected that he still wanted to know what was happening, what decisions had been made, and what was about to happen when staff were going to change his position or care for him in any manner.

In retrospect, I would have given him at least the slightest taste—just wetting his lips with lemonade. Knowing how easily aspiration can occur was present in my mind, not allowing me to stretch the chance that it would be okay. Then the questions started flowing in my mind: Would I want to taste my birthday cake and risk aspirating *or* not taste my birthday cake and totally avoid what could be a traumatic event? I did not want to take the risk of causing more pain, but which pain—the pain of denial or the pain of medical repercussion? That question lingered for a long time.

I am a calculated risk taker. Not frivolous; I will weigh the odds. I wanted D to have a silver lining that day. If you asked me what I would have done in retrospect, I believe he would have had the slightest of tastes, even if it was just to wet his lips with lemonade.

An Anniversary Celebration

Our nineteenth year of wedded experience was fast approaching. How would I make this meaningful?

At this point, D was unable to talk other than in an inaudible whisper. I had tried getting an amplifier to increase the volume, but it really didn't make a difference. I wanted so much to know what he was trying to say. What might he be wanting? What might I do for him that would make a difference?

On occasion, I would notice a very faraway look in his eyes, and being aware of the Alzheimer's, there was a time…no, maybe two, that I said to him, "D, do you know who I am?" If eyes could talk, his did, and what they said to me was, "Sloan, what kind of a question is that?" Now, that was a silver lining.

What I decided to do was to buy a luxurious version of the book, *My Utmost for His Highest*, written in a format for daily reading. I also bought a bookmark that was actually a cutout bouquet of a dozen red roses. Thus, a journey within a journey began. I showed D what I had gotten us for our anniversary, letting him know the bookmark of roses was his gift to me and that we would read a section each day together, which we did.

One day particularly stands out in my mind. As I finished reading one of the devotionals, I was not sure what the author was actually wanting to relay, so I turned to D as if all was very normal and asked him if he knew, explaining that I wasn't certain. To my amazement, he moved his head up and down. I said to him that I thought that was wonderful and he tried to say something, but I was never able to understand. When D tried to talk, he would move his lips as if whispering, but without definition, with his eyes often closed, or he would look off somewhere and become fixated, usually on the ceiling. At the same time, he would often do a semi-contained stretch with his arms, almost like a diversion.

Oh Lord, I wanted to cry, *how … how can this be happening?* I did cry when I reached my car and all the way home. I remember getting into bed that evening feeling so isolated, so alone, so weary. I did not see this as a meltdown because I wanted to cry; I didn't mind acknowledging my pain, and so I did.

By sunlight, I was ready to face yet another day.

A One-way Conversation

I arrived one early afternoon at the nursing home. One of the nurses said that D had shared a few words with her. Oh, how I wished it had been me. I went hopefully into his room but was greeted by no response. When I went back out into the hallway, the same nurse asked me if he said anything, to which I answered, "No. There is no response." The nurse came back into the room saying something to D about not saying anything to his wife and how dedicated I was to him and that he needed to respond to me. Did he know? Did he understand what this lovely nurse was suggesting?

My mind started searching—searching for what he might be feeling. The main thing that occurred to me was how much I knew he would like to be at home. Once he was lifted into a wheel chair, I took him for a walk around the community, which we often did. We would stop along the way and view different events and scenery. Sometimes, weather permitting, we would venture out into the courtyard. He liked to sit on the bridge and watch the turtles swimming around, which he had expressed an interest in back during his first week at Gwynedd.

When we arrived back to D's room a couple of hours later, I had made a decision about what was reeling around in my mind all afternoon. Since D could not communicate, if there was an issue that was causing pain, any resolve would have to come from me—solely me. With much trepidation, I started relaying to D how much it mattered to me that he get the very best care possible. That all along I had tried to make the right decisions regarding his care and was so sorry if they were not in harmony with his desires. That I knew he would like to be at home, but that financially, I needed to be working. And that to have the kind of care at home that he needed around the clock was not financially possible. I regretted that, but I was doing the best I knew how and wanted him to know each decision was about him, his needs, his well-being, and hopefully some peace of mind for each of us.

I proceeded to put my arms around him; I saw a hint of tear. I told him I loved him·and that it was okay for him to hug me back if he wanted to. As well as speech issues, D was almost totally immobile, not even being able to raise his hand to touch his face. Anyway, as I held him, I felt a hand touch my arm: an affectionate touch. A slight cloud was lifted. *No*, a silver lining appeared.

I was cognizant of the fact that when one cannot voice an opinion, when one cannot do anything to take care of their own personal needs, they are truly at the mercy of those around them. When I would play a CD, I would think, *Is this something he would like to hear? Maybe so, but how about now?* Or when I put the TV on, thinking it would give some interest to his environment, did he want peace and quiet instead? There were endless scenarios.

I always tried to communicate in a manner that would not cause him any anxiety in that he was not able to respond. I would ask first when wanting to do something for him, but I rarely got a response. Did no response mean, "No, I don't want that," or was the ability to respond just not present to any degree? Could he have given me some indication and just preferred to be totally disengaged? I must admit there were times I questioned.

This brings to mind that a few months before D's passing, a very good, lifelong friend of his died. I was torn whether to share this information. Would it create an anguish he would have to keep inside, unable to share with another? Before determining how I wanted to handle that, I discovered someone else had relayed the message to him. That's all I know; I was not there to observe a response if, in fact, there even was one.

The *big* questions often came down to, *What do I believe D would want?* and when that was not clear to me, *What would I want under the same circumstances?* Not that that was the gold standard, but it was my measuring guideline.

Shaving Away One's Beard and Mustache

D was impeccably well groomed, whether going into the courtroom or to the Penn Relays. It was a part of who he was. He would often say that he was as comfortable in a shirt and tie as anything else.

Every week at Gwynedd, I would shave D and trim his hair. Shaving was not the easiest task, as he had a very refined pattern for his mustache and beard, so I asked a young man from our church to come in and take care of that area of D's care, including his haircut. I had actually been cutting his hair for a number of years, off and on, mostly if we were in a hurry, going somewhere and time had not prevailed for him to go to the Men's Country Club. I loved doing it. No, it was not an unfulfilled ambition to have a salon. I could almost imagine a smile from D when another source arrived.

It was decided, because of different secretions, that it would be a good idea to get rid of the mustache and beard. In nineteen years, I had never seen D without a beard or mustache. I was certain to let him know we would be giving him a clean shave and asked if he could let me know if that was okay. I can only say it felt like he was saying okay, but that is with a very big question mark.

When completed, I did tell him how handsome he looked. I know, I know … It was my way of wanting to foster encouragement as I held the mirror for him to see the results. And he was handsome. There really wasn't much of a response, but I did notice his eyes scanning the mirror. The level of vulnerability just tugged at my heart. Every now and then, I would just have to ask, *Why? Why, Lord? Why* was not a question I normally asked; I just trusted. But on a rare occasion, the words were just simply present. This was one of those few *why* moments.

The Male Chorus–Last Words

There are ministries and there are ministries. The Siloam Male Chorus from our church won my heart in a big way. They would come and visit D, frequently making it a practice session. He was a member of their group.

What always amazed me was long after D had stopped talking per se, he would still have moments of singing along with the Male Chorus. I used to query if this was somehow a rote response. I had become well aware years before that songs enticed learning with repetition, and I knew from my own experiences after listening to a CD a number of times I would automatically know what was coming next even after I had not heard it for ages. There are a number of things in our lives that fall into this category, like typing, riding a bike, and reciting poetry, just to name a few.

Regardless of what allowed for that response, it pulled at my heartstrings. I never wanted to miss a practice, for it gave me the opportunity to see D sing and hear his voice. Seeing him sing made me imagine a lighter spirit. What a wonderful feeling that was. For one who trusted in the Lord as D, I like to believe there was still hope for the glorious life awaiting him.

Earlier in his stay at Gwynedd, before he stopped communicating totally, I wrote this note to the Male Chorus after their first visit.

> To all the special souls in our Male Chorus,
>
> What a wonderful visit you shared with D. His best therapy yet! I thank you so very much. D does, too. I'm going to share a conversation he and I had right after you all left. Hopefully, it will express to you his joy beyond that which you saw.
>
> I said, "Honey, you were singing!"
>
> D replied, "I was?"
>
> I said, "Yes, you were, and that was so exciting, and the Male Chorus said they would be coming back."
>
> D questioned, "How soon?"
>
> I replied, "I'm not sure, but I trust they will be back."
>
> D asked, "Where? When?"
>
> So you see, you warmed two hearts and shared God's hope, and we say together that we love you, applaud your ministry, and welcome you any time . . .
>
> Sloan

Whenever I knew the Male Chorus was singing, I made every attempt to be present, long after D's demise. I felt such an allegiance to their dedication.

One Sunday, as they were celebrating their anniversary, I was surprised when during their Ministry Moment, I was approached where I was, sitting in the back of the church, and escorted to the front of the church to join the Chorus. *Not in song*, thank heavens, for I have never been able to carry a tune, as much as I love music. Instead, they talked about my being an inspiration and presented me with a beautiful bouquet of roses. Oh, I was overwhelmed—this was *their* anniversary. I proceeded to share with them that it was their ministry that was inspiring, showing such dedication and love. What I would never forget was that, to my knowledge, the last words I ever heard D say, no, *sing* or say, was a short stanza to one of his favorite songs. "Heaven is a Beautiful Place."

Mother and Son

We had a wonderful duet (mother and son) ministry team from our church that had a ministry at Gwynedd, where D was, at 1:00 every first Sunday. I was excited about that, for it meant I could still attend a church service with him. It had been some time, but we hardly ever missed a Sunday for years, not until he was no longer able.

One of the first times we went, D kept his eyes closed the whole time. How much I wanted him to see who was there and perhaps feel the experience on a very personal level, with a degree of acknowledgment, which I believe did occur on one of the three Sundays we went. There were only three, for on the third Sunday, I could see him fighting tears—the pain of his situation too intense to acknowledge, if I dare to analyze.

The lesson here for me was that we can never assume what another is thinking or feeling; while that does not seem like a profound thought, I suspect it is something we all do more than we would like to admit or more than we are even aware of. It is very difficult not to ascribe a thought or feeling to another's actions when you are closely involved.

A Ride to Look at Christmas Lights

This was a most treasured moment. I wish there had been time for another such encounter.

We decided to rent a wheelchair van and take D out to see the Christmas lights. Just the thought of taking him out caused me to feel excited. *And,* he had motioned an affirmative when asked. So in December of 2006, on a cool night, my son, Stephen, daughter-in-law, Kim, and I arrived to take D out for a ride. His children were unable to make it, but his daughter wanted to pay for the event, which was so helpful. You may not realize, but renting a van can be expensive.

In the beginning, D had his eyes closed most of the time, as he did while we were getting him ready for this special little venture. As I observed him, I was praying this was something that would have a positive meaning for him, but to this point, he was not even looking. My heart sank. This goes back to what I was saying earlier about thinking for another. How accurate can we be? How wrong can we be?

As we would pull up to the houses, we realized that D could not turn his head to view the lights. My son would have to position the car so D could view the lights from a straightforward angle. About halfway into the trip, D's eyes were still not open, so I said to D, "Sweetheart, I want to share with you that Tracey was so enthused about your getting out to see the lights that she is paying for our adventure. Isn't that wonderful?" With that, he leaned in my direction and smiled a very heartwarming, definable smile. It made the whole evening worthwhile; more than that, as we continued on our trip, which we extended, D was looking at most of the lights from that point on. I could see his eyes taking it all in.

I had learned to read D's eyes. It is amazing how when certain senses/abilities diminish, others become keener, not only for the one with the loss, but for the one closely attuned. It's a part of our Lord's wonderful plan. We are so blessed to be a part of this wonderful human race.

As we were saying goodnight to D, I asked him if he would like to do that again sometime, and he moved his head slightly, ever so slightly, up and down. I trusted that it had been a good experience for him. If only we could have done it one more time. *If only just one more time.*

Just getting him out was *huge*. I must admit, during our adventure, I wanted to take him by our home, but I remembered that previous experience we had and decided that in his condition that would not be fair. Second-guessing, huh? What else was there to do?

A New Year's Eve Party

What could possibly make this an event one to savor, one to remember, one with meaning? I am one who sees the possibilities as limitless. For me, it is a matter of being resourceful and then, last but not least, it is how I chose to view it.

Just before the party started, we had a most welcomed visit from our special cousins, wanting to wish us a happy New Year. That was a wonderful start to our upcoming event. Gwynedd created the perfect backdrop.

As I wheeled D into the main dining room, I could feel excitement well up within as I viewed the tables neatly set up with linen tablecloths and service ware that looked like crystal, including dishes for snacks and cookies and champagne glasses for toasting in the New Year with bubbling apple cider. There was long-loved music provided by a couple musicians that was just right for dancing (perhaps a fox trot), and the staff were all dressed up as if attending a formal affair. People were singing, and wheel chairs were moving around the floor as if in dance, even D's, with me leading for the first time, and the smiles—the smiles were contagiously everywhere.

The event ended with "Auld Lang Syne," and everyone returned to their respective rooms with some sense of inner pleasure. I don't really know that for sure, but what I do know is the difference in the expression I observed from patient to patient, those who I would see every day as I came to and fro in the Gwynedd environment. Even D, who, for the most part, had been expressionless for some time, exhibited a slightly softer expression. I went home that evening sensing a lighter spirit than I had in some time; we had brought in the New Year together. There was no sense of what that meant or would look like; it was simply living in the here and now, something I was becoming rather proficient at doing. What really mattered was simply this moment.

Thank You, Hospice

What is hospice? I didn't know. For some reason, I thought it was a place, as I had no previous exposure. When I say that now, it is hard for me to believe I ever thought that, but I have been surprised by the number of others who have thought the same thing.

The aspects of hospice are far-reaching, in our case, providing volunteers to come in during the day while I was at work to bring some stimulation into D's life. They would take him around in his wheel chair, read to him, play music for him, and play the piano and sing for him, as well as meet any need they saw while there. They would work in adjunct with the nursing staff, providing activity that a nursing staff really isn't expected to do. Once hospice was called in, it meant that D would no longer be taking any medicine to prolong his existence as it was, but just that which would provide comfort in the process. They also provided insight and literature to the family regarding each different behavior that might be observed as one nears the end of their earthly life.

Hospice can be brought in on a case even if death is not considered imminent within a short period of time.

Each three months, the case is reevaluated and deemed either appropriate or not for hospice care. We had one such evaluation.

Hospice serves not only the infirmed, but also those whose lives are connected. The comfort they can bring to such a situation can be incredible.

I urge you to never overlook the possibilities that are available to you in any given situation.

A Book of Happenings

So Many Loving Authors

One day, as I arrived at Gwynedd, I noticed a journal-like book with a pen attached on the night table next to D's bed. I went over, picked it up, and was delightfully surprised when I noticed two messages within. One was from the friend who brought it in and one was from a hospice volunteer, each one depicting their visit with D to share with me. It gave me a glimpse of his days beyond what I could possibly know as I worked in my office, anticipating the arrival of 5:00 p.m.

What I learned is that things are not always what they seem. Oh yes, I knew that, but confirmation was occurring. I also learned that little things mean a lot. I knew that, too. I had further confirmation that within the most simple of renderings could be a spectacular benefit. More silver linings!

This special little journal served another purpose as well. Visitors would often write a message as if they were talking with D, and I would anxiously look for a time when he would seem alert to be sure and read the messages. Some were very touchingly directed to him, with the comment that the author was not certain D would ever know what had been written. When I read the messages, I would always let the person who wrote it know, and I certainly would share any response I observed.

On occasion, I could see his eyes moving in a manner that told me he was hearing and, I believe, taking in the words, thoughts, and feelings I was sharing through others' written words. There could be times when D would seem totally disengaged, but other times, you would sense his attention and would seize those times to share.

In many of these instances, for certain, if the sentiments had been just spoken instead of written, he would have missed the wonderful, caring messages. This process also gave those visiting the hope that he would somehow come to know what they would have liked him to know.

This little book had many special nuggets. When I know one who is in similar circumstances, this is now my gift to them.

The following are some of the treasured entries of the journal.

To maintain each correspondent's privacy, where a name is used within a quote, I have used the letter Z for designation.

Excerpts

A note from a loving son—

I came to see Dad today. He spoke to me briefly when I put some new music on. Mostly he was asleep, but it was just good to be here with him.

A note from a loving nephew—

…I stopped by to visit, but you were sound asleep…sorry I did not get to speak to you. I'm looking at pictures from your birthday on the wall poster…You were looking good in your bright blue colors…I love you, take care.

A note from a loving uncle—

…I just felt the urge to come and visit. You were asleep. I wanted you to know that I love you.

A note from a loving brother—

Even though you have not said a word or given me an indication that you are aware of my presence, it is nevertheless comforting for me to be able to sit with you in silence. I've said a prayer for you and will continue to do so. The following have asked about you…you are blessed and loved.

A note from a loving niece—

Happy New Year! Z and I came to pray with you and offer our love. May God continue to hold you in His hands.

Another note from niece—

It was a blessing to hear that the two of you enjoyed the garden today! Thank you God...My mom and I stopped by, but D was asleep and we didn't want to wake him. D, you look good in your burgundy shirt...May God continue to bless you...

Another note from niece—

Z and I send our love. D was asleep, but we prayed with him.

A note from a long-time and very special friend—

Dear Mr. Rogers, It's me, Z. I came by to visit since I had a vacation day. I didn't bring Z with me because I wanted you all to myself! Sitting here with you makes me realize how much I miss you...I couldn't stop thinking about the ways you influenced my life. Thank you for allowing me to occupy a special place in your heart!...while my earthly father had passed away a long time ago, I didn't realize then that my heavenly father had placed you in my life.

(After recounting many special memories, she continued—)

...Out of all these memories, the most precious and meaningful time was when I gave you a ride home from the office and before you went inside, we prayed together. How special and marvelous it was to pray with and for a man that means so much to me … As I leave you today, I will read to you, Psalm 23. Until next time … Z.

[I don't know if she knew this to be his favorite scripture]

A note from a church/family friend who shared the same birth date—

God has not forsaken you … As I spoke to you today, I know you understood who I was and what I said.

A poem by a church friend—
Roses are red, violets are blue,
God seeked you out to help us get over
being blue and our problems, too.
Roses are red, violets are blue,
We have come unselfishly to show our gratitude
Roses are red, violets are blue,
You have seen many of our lives
designated to change for the better by you
Roses are red, violets are blue,
Only God's infinite wisdom in his heart
can and will carry you through
Roses are red, violets are blue,
You are the best in whatever
decisions you set out the challenge to do.

From a church friend, who is since deceased—
One of the greatest blessings God can give us is the gift of a friend who cares. Thank you for being that friend. With Love.

Another note from since deceased friend—

Dick opened his eyes when I spoke to him. He kept them open for a little while.

Thanks for the beautiful card, D looks good in my picture.

[I had taken a picture of each of D's birthday guests with D and sent them a copy to have and to hold.]

Another note from since deceased friend—

Have not seen you in awhile. Wanted you to know that I am praying for and thinking about you...

From church friends—

Z and I came by to say hello to Deacon Rogers and you... Deacon Rogers knows that we are here. We had prayer with him...

These following nuggets were from hospice for me—

...I was in to see D today. He was wide awake and looking out the window when I arrived...I didn't get much response...

...I was here yesterday at 1:00 p.m., and we read, *Walking with the Shepherd*.

...I read to D and massaged his hands. I will say a prayer with him before I leave...

...we also took a walk in the courtyard. Z had him in his wheel chair. His eyes were wide open when outside in the garden. I put him to bed at 1:30 p.m.

...I helped Z get D washed and dressed again today. I lotioned his hands and will be reading more of *Walking with the Shepherd*.

… not responsive today.

… D was at Halloween party. Brought him back. Put radio on and read church letter to him. Was responsive today; eyes opened when I made sounds.

… eyes open, no response when I spoke to him.

… helped with his transfer to wheel chair. I walked him around halls and stopped in activities room. Listened to music and looked out at garden.

… Hi, Sloan. I haven't seen D in awhile. I'll massage D's hands and read more from *Walking with the Shepherd*.

… I am here this morning … to assist getting D out of bed.

Mr. Rogers is awake, opened eyes and tries to converse after stimulation … Going to sing along with eyes open and listening …

… Hello, my name is Z. I spent an hour here today to keep D company. I wheeled him around the facility, sang to him, and played hymns and Christmas Carols on the organ, hoping he heard them. I said a prayer with him and I am keeping you both in daily prayer …

… Richard was in bed napping when I arrived so there was no trip to the room with the organ. Instead, I sang to him and read Psalms and the Christmas story from Luke.

The last entry—

1/9/07. I spent 45 min. today with D reading to him from *Christ in our Home*. We covered a lot of ground as I wheeled him several times around the facility.

Even though the changes in D's condition were minute, this gave me an opportunity to *see*, to share vicariously in the events of D's day, while having to be at work. It was the next best thing to being physically present. It was a means for compassionate, eager hearts to share in a most profound way!

Compassion From All Around

Hundreds of Kind, Kindred Hearts

Compassion—that special ingredient that creates mental and physical hugs. How can we live without them? It hurts to think that there are those who do; no one should.

Compassion—that special ingredient that is expressed in caring and knowing words of sympathy and empathy.

Compassion—that special ingredient that creates kind acts that are intended from heartfelt interest and concern.

I learned that compassion and caring for another can come in all forms. There were times when a phone call, a visit, an e-mail, a special poem, a book, or a card, to name a few, appeared at a time that gave me incredible strength for a needed moment. *So* I say, if you are lead to reach out, just do it, do not put it off. Look at it as a vessel that God has chosen to reach another in need. Trust me, that is how it works. That's how God wants it to work. That's how God wants you to work. First Peter 3:8 says, "Be ye all of one mind, having compassion one of another."

Remember those silver linings I mentioned? See how they can add up. Plus, there is that special element in our lives I relate to as "in God's time—God's perfect timing." The Lord knows our needs; He knows when we need that special sustenance. We will either be a receiver or a giver if we only respond to our heart's direction; that's where God touches us, you know, within our hearts. There are times we will be the recipient, needing that special touch, and there are times when we will be the supplier if we just listen to our hearts and acknowledge the moment.

How about reaching out in conversation? I learned as well that when we tell another we would like to help and ask what that person needs or wants, it may not be enough. In times of stress or trauma, one often doesn't know what it is that they need or even want, other than to survive the event they are facing. So trust your instincts, for we often already know what will make another feel better.

There may be times we may not be able to meet an actual need as perceived, but we can remain present with a word of hope and encouragement. A word of hope and encouragement is acknowledgment of another's situation, their pain, their discontent, and their concerns, giving them the opportunity to just talk. It might be a suggestion to help them move forward in a new direction or to evaluate other options. Be creative. If you believe you can help, ideas will present themselves.

You might want to give some time. Time is so precious to each of us that even when we are not busy we tend to guard our time. One might say that is all the more reason. However, think of the gift you share when you say to one who is traumatized with challenging events, "Take an hour or two and I will be here in your place for you," *or* "Let me do that for you so that you can stay focused on where you need to be right now."

When I had the thyroid biopsies, it was my sister Raina, who made all the necessary arrangements to make certain that the cultures were sent to and reviewed by Sloan Kettering, Thomas Jefferson, and John's Hopkins. As much as I understood the importance and would have had to find a way to make it happen, just having that burden lifted at a time when I was confronted with so many other draining issues meant more to me than words will ever describe.

And, I can't forget Raina and Stephen accompanying me for the thyroid biopsies—a very grueling procedure, particularly to one who cannot tolerate Novocain and who is somewhat emotionally drained by life's circumstances. Imagine thirteen needle extractions from existing cysts through the neck. Not a delicate needle; it had to be large enough to extract tissue. Raina and Stephen were my numbing agents, whose support allowed me to see it through.

I was grateful for every kind word and deed. Regardless of its magnitude, it was something I never took for granted. I viewed each kindness as a gift from the heart and not one I automatically deserved or expected. Perhaps that is why there was such strength attached to each action that was shared with me.

When we take something for granted, it simply does not carry the same weight or have the same impact as when we see it as a special gift, intended with heartfelt compassion. Similarly, do not prejudge the value of your action. There were times when a phone call or card meant as much to me as what might be perceived as a more major act.

Please, as a part of reaching out, never forget the power of prayer. *Every prayer counts. Every prayer*! When I was fighting for my life after an aneurysm, prayer lines were orchestrated across the country by my wonderful sister—one who understands the power of prayer—and others as the process started. There were hundreds of people, who I will never know, praying for me. How awesome is that? Such compassion!

There were those who cared enough to take their time to pray for me, a fellow being, someone they didn't know and would never know, except for a glimpse of being informed of another's need. Prayer works miracles. Not only did I survive a major subarachnoid hemorrhage, but regained my memory just in time to comment on medicine I was being given. It was upon my questioning that the mistake was recognized, or I would have received the wrong medication; who knows what the outcome would have been?

Have you ever experienced an earthly angel, one who touches your life in an extremely profound way? From the moment I arrived at the hospital by ambulance, an emergency room nurse announced to my family that she would be taking care of me and was not going to let anything or anyone get in the way of her getting me through this event. She didn't leave my side.

Why do I tell you this story? I view it as an example of God's presence, his all-knowing presence.

Without a doubt, prayers were answered. Without a doubt, compassion continued.

When I was out of work and looking for employment, there were many who knew my need and directed all kinds of possibilities my way. As I mentioned previously, that is when I recognized the importance of God's timing. He knows what you and I could never hope to have total grasp of. If we learn to lean on him with a trusting and grateful heart, what we need will be lovingly supplied.

Imagine, we do not have to worry about *if* or *when*. Sounds impossible, doesn't it? I agree. "*Sounds*" is the operative word here. Are you familiar with the time-old adage, "Things are not always what they seem to be"? Just because it sounds impossible, doesn't make it so. This brings to mind a favorite saying of mine: *Esse quam videri*, "To be, rather than to appear."

Do not ever make a personal judgment that you don't deserve God's goodness. God has more grace than you could ever imagine. It is easier to recognize God's wonderful, endless grace when we ourselves extend grace. This is similarly related in the Lord's Prayer, which so beautifully says "…forgive us our trespasses as we forgive those who trespass against us." The power in those words is unbelievable. Can you know personal peace any other way?

Below is a thank-you note for a bouquet of flowers sent to me after D's passing, a note that speaks to the compassion of others.

ACTS Retirement-Life Communities, Inc. is my employer, and how blessed I am.

> To all my friends and employees at ACTS:
>
> Some time has passed since Dick's passing, but not the gratefulness.
>
> I feel in my heart for each shared response.
>
> In my search for employment, I was lead to ACTS at a most important/challenging time in my life. There was no question, as the days went on, that it was orchestrated by God.
>
> At first, I was so relieved that where I would be working was just around the corner from where Dick would spend the next eight months. I had experienced many months in the past where to visit Dick in health facilities would be an hour's ride each way, each day. However, my gratefulness reaches much further than that.
>
> In no way could I have anticipated the awesome number of caring hearts and support that awaited me. *And* in no way could I have found the strength to endure, in the same way, without so many heartfelt expressions.
>
> The beautiful bouquet of flowers sent to my home was a constant reminder, when my heart was

so sad, that in a special corner of my life there were those wanting to lighten my burden, and you did.

Each prayer, each card, each visit at Dick's viewing, each hug, each shared word of encouragement has brightened my path and given me incredible hope for the future.

What a perfect example that when you are on a painful/difficult journey, blessings still flow.

I will be forever thankful.

Sloan

I was told that those in the board meetings prayed for both D and me many times during those long months. How often would you expect that to happen in your work environment? I was in awe. How could I not have been?

Another thing I realize is that regardless of one's faith or belief structure, there is something very comforting about prayer. When one is traumatized or distraught over any matter, prayer can reach a soul—almost any soul, even those who refute it—in an unbelievable way. When we feel helpless, just think, from where can hope be derived? How many times have you heard one say, "I'll try anything"?

My work environment brought about other acts of compassion. It was through a very caring senior vice president of quality care that I was directed to understand the full workings of hospice and that they were there for all terminal-type illnesses, not just ones of a specific nature. At that juncture, never having had any experience with hospice, I didn't realize it is a service that comes to you, whether at home, in a hospital, or nursing-type home. I learned enough to recognize I wanted to make hospice a part of D's care. It was an instant decision that got an instant response. I was grateful.

A co-worker, whose friendship I have come to value immensely and who is our hospice administrator, actually came out to visit D with me shortly before his passing. In her quick meeting of him, she gave me some wonderful insight as to often-predictable stages of one's passing. This gave clarity to what was happening, what I was observing.

Involving hospice is a wonderful way for a caregiver to feel some reprieve. They give extra care, extra insight, extra activity involvement, and extra support that all spells e-x-t-r-a c-o-m-p-a-s-s-i-o-n.

When it comes to compassion, many coworkers have listened to me, prayed with and for me, hugged me, and even shed a momentary tear. The senior vice president of sales and marketing, who I worked directly for, gave me a special gift, the peace of knowing that I could leave with a moment's notice, should a need arise. The list of kind and caring acts from ACTS could go on and on.

At this point, I wonder if you might be thinking of things you have done in a reach-out mode or things you have received from another reaching out to you. Perhaps you are realizing that the elements of compassion are far-reaching.

Compassion is the action of an empathetic heart.

> Helen Keller, at the age of nineteen wrote, "So long as you can sweeten another's pain, life is not in vain."

Dear children, let's not merely say that we love each other; let us show the truth by our actions.

1 John 3:18 (NLT)

Finally, all of you, live in harmony with one another; be sympathetic, love as brothers, be compassionate and humble.

1 Peter 3:8 (NIV)

Faith Prevails— Walking with the Shepherd

Strength's Source

Who better to lead our footsteps, who better to hold our hand, who better to share our heart's pain, than our shepherd, Jesus!

As you think back over the years or maybe just hours, is there something in your life you lean on when you are at your lowest ebb, *or* perhaps something you give special attention to on an everyday basis, just because it brings you hope?

Might it be a special coin you rub between your fingers? How about a smooth stone with a special, encouraging word you roll over and over again in your hand? How about a beautiful seashell you discovered unexpectedly in the surf? I guess the list could go on and on. For D, it was a very special and beautiful rendition of Psalm 23, called *Walking with the Shepherd*, which augmented his faith.

At one point it became a necessary reading for me. Anything that could have that degree of impact for one I cared about, how could I not want to share that special ingredient in his life? Even though we both proclaimed our strong faith in our Lord, we each had our way of deriving strength from our belief, prayer being front and foremost.

Walking with the Shepherd became an integral part of D's life—not the book, but the message. While he carried the book with him most frequently, he read it, studied it, savored it, and yes, devoured every word to grasp its full impact. It was such a part of D that it accompanied him on his final earthly journey.

What one might derive from this wonderful portrayal:

The Lord is my Shepherd: I shall not want...

- Do we know his presence as we know our own?
- Do we *trust* him explicitly as our comfort and strength at all times?

He makes me to lie down in green pastures; He leads me beside the still waters...

- Do we have comfort within our own being, unrelated to another?

- Are we finding blessings where we are because we have turned to God?

- What are the gifts supporting our lives right now and have we given thanks for them?

- Are we giving love as well as receiving it?

He restores my soul; He leads me in the paths of righteousness for His name's sake...

- Our awareness of God's presence is based on truth and self-discovery.

- Are we expressing our faith in a way that encourages others as we grow together by facing daily challenges experiencing grace?

- Are we using our leisure time to restore our bodies and minds?

- "Truly my soul silently waits for God: from Him comes my salvation" (Psalms 62:1).

Yea, though I walk through the valley of the shadow of death, I will fear no evil; for You are with me; Your rod and Your staff, they comfort me...

- Can we let go and let God? This shows immeasurable trust.

- Are we too proud to be carried by the Lord? Are we too sick and powerless not to be? Are we humiliated at needing help or joyful at its presence?

- Do we see ourselves as ones who can encourage others to follow the path between our earthly life and eternity and to realize it is just an extension of where we are now?

- Or, to help other Davids defeat Goliaths and glorify God, one who never changes. (Remember, Goliaths can be circumstances)

You prepare a table before me in the presence of my enemies...

- Do we seek God so we will have a greater capacity to love and be loved?

- Do we know how others view us? What do we see when we look in the mirror?

- Are we working on forgiveness, which is necessary to create that greater connection with our Lord that leads to a greater love for all?

You anoint my head with oil; my cup runs over...

- How can we share the oil of brightness with others each day?

Surely, goodness and mercy shall follow me all the days of my life...

- Though our strength grows, we should never deny God's guidance.

- Do we stay attuned to that still small voice of God?

- Do we know that God's mercy and goodness are with us even when we have to make painful decisions?

- Can we view our doubts and roadblocks as happenings that make us more compassionate in our love for another?

And I will dwell in the house of the Lord forever.

- Are we living a full and abundant life, one that will sustain us from now and into eternity?

Know the Lord, and you will know peace.

The Twenty-Third Psalm, A Psalm of David (NKJV):

The Lord is my shepherd;
I shall not want.
He makes me to lie down in green pastures;
He leads me beside the still waters.
He restores my soul;
He leads me in the paths of righteousness
For His name's sake.
Yea, though I walk through the valley
of the shadow of death,
I will fear no evil;
For You are with me;
Your rod and Your staff,
they comfort me.
You prepare a table before me in the
presence of my enemies;
You anoint my head with oil;
My cup runs over.
Surely goodness and mercy shall
follow me
All the days of my life;
And I will dwell in the house
of the Lord
Forever.

The Death Before Dying

Have I Really Lost You?

You are gone, deprived of the ability to share. I see you and do not hear you. I see you and can't feel your touch. My heart longs. My heart reconciles.

We have all experienced loss to one degree or another; it is a recognizable part of life.

When we lose one to an illness before their death, have we really lost them? For me, I recognized the loss in stages, many stages, until the time came that there was no meaningful communication. At one time I might have told you that even no communication is communication, and I would still say that in some circumstances, but I don't believe so when it is not of your own volition.

When you watch one trying to utter words and, at best, there may be a faint whisper or a trying to respond to a desire to touch and they are unable to, you begin to realize how much of a loss has ensued. It is a major loss for the person who is debilitated as well as a loss for those looking on. While you try to minimize that loss, the void calls out to you. It resounds in your heart. You long to attach something of meaning to the absence of anything. Try as you may, reality calls out to you, painfully, mercilessly, until acceptance takes hold.

All decisions came from me as much as I wanted D to be a part of what was impacting him, all conversation was one-way, all affection was given by me, never again to be received. What else was there? A momentary look was, for the most part, expressionless, with amazement of what you tried to read into that ray of contact. But, you move on, knowing you can't make it different. You can't make it something it is not. When do you stop trying? Do you stop? Do you even want to stop?

I was determined to bring D's world as much to life as possible. Even though he was not able to respond, I still conversed, telling him about my day, telling him any news he might care about, and painting verbal pictures. I read from the journal messages addressed to him very frequently, trusting he heard what I was saying on behalf of each caring author.

One thing that was a plus for D, and I encourage you to consider if you have a loved one in nursing care away from home, was a large-sized poster board filled with pictures of family and friends and a couple large pictures of his grandchildren hung separately. I would occasionally see him observing these prints, knowing it was the next best thing to their presence. The poster board was born out of pictures from his birthday party at Gwynedd.

Earlier on in our journey at Gwynedd, I did try to see if I could develop a means of communication through writing. I had gotten a large board with felt-tip markers and was crushed when I realized D could not even write his name. I was certain I had found a path to venture down. Another hope dashed. I just wanted to hold him and protect him from the world. Another grandiose thought, huh? Oh well, I guess we are entitled from time to time.

Not only was conversation and any substitute means to communicate missing, all reciprocal affection was gone as well. I remember placing my hand under D's to feel like it was being held or taking his hand in mine to massage. There was little response early on, to where I was not certain if it was of decision or involuntary, for it was so minimal. Was it something he did not want, was it something he could not face, or was it something he did not have the ability to respond to? Regardless, at that point, you just make it what you would hope it to be, what you quietly pray for. At least that is what I did.

Then there is your world at home—a place that has become one you realize your spouse (in this instance) will never return to, though his life hovers close by. As I spent most of my time working or spending time with D and making sure his needs were being met, I was home very little. When I was, I lost myself in the TV. Now, you would have to know me to understand what a huge statement that is. When I met D, I did not own a TV, by choice. That is not to say I didn't recognize there are some good programs on TV, but I always had other interests that kept me busy or were just simply more important. However, it seemed there was something about watching TV that got me away from myself.

Did I feel like D was already gone? Yes, in most ways, he was. *And* I can still hear myself saying, "I've already lost D." However, in retrospect, I really hadn't lost him, in that my life was still revolving around his every need. It was imperative to me to make sure his every need was being taken care of in the best possible manner, even if by others, and that I stay in touch with his presence through one-way conversation. Even though I could not hear him, he could hear me.

We were relating heart-to-heart.

I had thought about naming this book, *The Death before Dying*, but changed my mind. There was no death before D's dying, just significant loss—major loss for D and sheer numbness that was overtaking me.

When I speak of numbness, I am not referring to loss of cognitive powers, but rather loss of emotional feelings. I had learned to move beyond the pain by changing its perspective, thus, the *Death before Dying*.

There was always hope. Even hope that one can move on beyond suffering and find peace in their eternal resting place does not diminish one single moment that remains.

To give full impact to the above words, I share with you an event at D's funeral. As a tradition in our church just before the service starts, the immediate family is ushered forth to view the deceased one last time. Part of that ritual is with the spouse, in this case, being given a small, fine, delicate cloth to cover your loved one's face. *This was finality.* I froze at the last moment despite the loving strength of my youngest son supporting me. Gratefully, my stepdaughter, in her gracious, beautiful style, saved the moment.

That was the moment—the moment that had *final* written all over it.

The Final
Farewell

*There is a Beginning and
There is an Earthly End*

I had a vision, a vision I still have not fully
comprehended but no longer feel the need
to. It was what it was, a moment in time,
the last moment, the last time.

On January 15, I went to Gwynedd at
lunchtime to visit with D, as I did each
day. There was something about him that
seemed brighter, no, *much* brighter than
usual. This was encouraging. I am not certain that is the right word. *Encouraging*

for what? That he would just keep going on in this state that was so disheartening, this state that he wanted to be relieved of being in long before it ever got to such a devastating point? I guess what I felt was that he appeared to be suffering less at moments like those. *And* perhaps, just perhaps, there might be a chance to share some communication; I longed for that. That's what mattered.

My spirit was definitely lighter as I almost skipped to my car. "Thank you, Lord," were my words as I prepared to drive out of the parking lot. I was relieved to the point that I decided to take an evening away from visiting and deliver a book to my friend and hurry home to pay bills. However, I did call before I turned my car away from Gwynedd to check with the nurse as to D's status. There was nothing of concern.

Do you have any idea of the energy that can go into making a left turn as opposed to a right turn? The mind is an interesting thing. The right turn would have given me one last evening with D. So was the left turn the wrong turn? You may have been asking yourself that; I would have been if I were you. My answer is clear that turning left that evening was not the wrong turn, for it was based on the knowledge I had at that given moment, and I will hold the brighter spirit I shared with D close in memory.

Regardless, it was still late when I got to bed that night. I awakened to my phone ringing somewhere around 4:00 a.m. and a nurse telling me that I needed to come, that D was not doing well.

I was dressed and out of the house in a few minutes, shaking as I hurriedly threw on the first thing my hands touched. Brushing my hair and applying makeup were not even in the thought process. I got in my car knowing I would make the necessary phone calls to children and siblings as I drove along, which I did. In the anxiety of the moment, I missed a turn and found myself having to compute a different route, which, I must tell you, did not come in a conscious format. I barely parked my car when I arrived at Gwynedd. I rang the bell, as the door locks at a certain time of evening. The nurse was there in seconds.

As I hurried down the hall to see my husband, I was not one hundred percent certain this was the end for him. During this long journey, we had lived through perhaps three similar calls with a slightly different twist, but you do get to where you realize it as a human call and God is the one in charge.

I remember once being led out of D's room to the nursing office to make calls to the family to tell them that D would not last through the night. This was several months earlier. I further recall, as I made the calls, relaying the information just as it was given, for the words were not resonating with my spirit. I remember shaking as I dialed each number, but not feeling certain, or perhaps the word should be "convinced," about the message I was sharing.

But here I was, on this bleak, January 16, 2007, at 4:30 in the morning, heading toward D's room.

As the nurse and I raced down the long hall, which seemed twice as long as usual, she shared with me that D had stopped breathing. Did I hear those words correctly? No, it couldn't be. I felt like I was going to stop breathing as well. She proceeded to tell me when he stopped breathing that she had told him I was on my way and to hang on just a little longer and he started breathing again. How I cherished the workings of our Lord.

Each moment counted, like pure gold. How long could D hold on? All I could say was, "Please Lord. Please Lord."

My heart was momentarily grateful, grateful that he had hung on. Should I be grateful that he was leaving his earthly residence? Yes, yes I should, for that meant no more suffering, it meant God was all loving and merciful, it meant that D's prayer was answered, it meant that D would be at peace. How could I not want that for him? But, how about the years we had spent together, the special moments we had shared, the families we had brought together, things hoped for, all of which tugged at my heart as well?

Now there was a twinge of how I would feel if this was truly *The Call*, a slight override from the numbness that had begun to take hold within my being. It is amazing to me the range of emotion that can appear in a given moment.

I recall when D was at Temple and we were told that he was not going to make it, walking out of the critical care area to the waiting room with my stepdaughter and saying to Tracey, "I am not going to lose you too, am I?"

How grateful I was that by that time I had developed relationships with my stepchildren that were authentic in their own right. Initially, when you bring families together, you reach out to your extended new family because of the love you have for the new person in your life. As time goes forward and your experiences increase, each person within that new family becomes special to you in their own way.

While this was the fourth time I was told D would not make it, it was the first time I received a call in the early-morning hours and the first time I was told he had stopped breathing.

D and I were starting the last hour and a half of our twenty-year journey of which you have just heard about the last six years. It was an hour and a half that seemed only seconds long.

Present in the room with me were my oldest son, D's youngest son, my twin sister, one of D's brothers, and my niece. D's daughter called in (she was on her way up from Maryland), and I was able to hold the phone to her father's ear for her to share her final sentiments. I was so grateful for that, as there was no way she could get there in time. D's oldest son had called but was also unable to arrive in time.

I wanted to stay strong for D, but I also wanted him to know it was so painful for our journey to be ending, especially as it was without exchange. I allowed myself to cry … no, no, I kind of cried, "Oh no, D!" as I observed his breathing becoming more and more sporadic. I knew I had truly received the final call. I knew it was real; it was real in my soul. *It was happening. Yes, it was happening.*

I sensed activity around me with those few close family members who had arrived, but I was in my own world at that moment, wanting to do something, and not even knowing what that was. For eight months now, D had been awaiting this moment. Here it was. He was ready, *was I?*

The nurse was coming in and out and apprising us of D's status. I don't think it mattered at that point. Oh, maybe it did. I was kind of frozen in the moment and everything else was peripheral.

D was moving on to eternity, something he had wanted for the last eight months, at least. Had I ever really let go? Had I ever told him it was okay? Maybe once, awkwardly, as it would have been a one-way conversation.

You know, when you work avidly to aid one in deriving the best of care with the most comfort possible, it is like you are on a mission. You are actually protecting that person, which does not put you in a frame of mind to let go. It is directly opposite to the protective energy flow, but D needed to know that now—not that it would change his time, but perhaps the peace with which he would move forward.

So D could hear, I prayed aloud, "Lord, please take D. Take my husband home with you and keep him in your ever-loving arms. Sweetheart, the Lord is with you, D. He has his arms around you. He will take care of you. We will all be fine. I love you, D. We all love you, and it is okay. It's okay to go in peace, D."

Then I had this glimpse of him sitting up, his eyes opened wide (which they hadn't been for months), staring straight into mine as if unable to shift focus; time stopped for a moment and then he took his last breath. I have no recollection of the next few moments, just the vision I described, etched in my mind. What puzzled me was that I envisioned him sitting up straight, and I don't think he was. I have received mixed messages as to that fact. Why does it matter? All I can say is at that given moment, each second, each aspect mattered.

Once I was told he was gone, I remember sitting at the edge of his bed, holding his hand in mine, trying to grasp the realness of this, our last moment together. If I held his hand really tightly, would it make a difference?

I was so focused on watching his chest in case it might rise again with an intake of air. But as the minutes ticked away, I knew, yes, I knew it was truly over as to his actual presence in my life. His last breath had been taken.

When D and I started our life together in marriage, it was as a threesome: D, me, and our Lord. We not only made our commitment to each other, but to God as well.

When D left this earthly existence, the same three were present: D, me, and our Lord.

D, you are at peace in our Father's arms, *and* you will dwell in the house of the Lord forever and ever.

There is a beginning and there is an earthly end.

From the Tree of Life
Each leaf must fall—
The green, the gold,
The great, the small,
Each one in God's own time
He'll call—
With perfect love
He gathered you, my dear.

—Anonymous

"For everything there is a season, and a time for every matter under heaven"

Ecclesiastes 3:1 (RSV)

Addendum

*Additional Ventures of
an Inspired Man*

For four decades, Dick supported the Montgomery County Association for the Blind as board president and solicitor, the Children's Aid Society of Montgomery County as a board member, the Opportunities Industrialization Center as a charter member, and the George Washington Carver Community Center, in Norristown, as solicitor, member, director, and board chairman.

Additionally, he served on the boards of a Southeastern Pennsylvania Chapter of the American Red Cross, the Visiting Nurses Association, the Norristown State Hospital, the Central Montgomery County Optimist Club of Norristown, Montgomery County District Board of Health and Welfare Council, Inc., The Montgomery County Advisory Committee for Eagleville Hospital and Montgomery County MH-MR Emergency Service.

His professional memberships included the American, the Pennsylvania, and Montgomery County Bar Associations; the Barrister Association of Philadelphia and the National Bar Association in Washington, D.C.; the Pennsylvania Trial Lawyers Association; and the American Arbitration Association.

He was a staunch supporter of the Montgomery County Democratic Party and briefly served as vice chair. He was also a member of the Norristown Lions Club and Alpha Phi Alpha Fraternity.

Other areas that Dick devoted time to were the Penn Relays (he was also a recognized runner), Million Man March, Promise Keepers, and NAACP, all of which he pursued until he was no longer able.